The Order of the Stick™

On the Origin of PCs

Written and Illustrated by
Rich Burlew

GIANT in the PLAYGROUND™

www.GiantITP.com

ISBN 0-9766580-1-1
ISBN-13: 978-0-9766580-1-6

Published by:
Giant in the Playground Games
2417 Welsh Road, Suite 21 #328
Philadelphia PA 19114
www. GiantITP.com
customerservice@GiantITP.com

Third printing: November 2006

New episodes of *The Order of the Stick* are available several times
each week for free at our website, **www.GiantITP.com**. If you have
the book, chances are you already knew that, but we figured we'd
cover all of the bases.

Also available from Giant in the Playground

Dungeon Crawlin' Fools
The Order of the Stick saga begins
here! Well, really, it begins in the
book you have in your hands, sort
of, but the first OOTS strips are in
this book. So, you should really
read this one first.

160 pages, color. $24.95

No Cure for the Paladin Blues
Out of the dungeon and into the
wilderness, the Order of the Stick
continues its quest in this second
compilation. Third book overall,
though, since this isn't technically
a "compilation" per se, as it doesn't
compile any existing material.

244 pages, color. $29.95

In cooperation with APE Games:

OOTS Adventure Game
This epic card-based board
game lets you take on the
role of one of the OOTS
members as you descend
ever deeper in search of the
most important reward of
all: bragging rights!

Over 500 cards. $39.95
Visit www.apegames.com for details

Preface by Redcloak

So it seems that I have been chosen to write the Preface here primarily because I don't have any scenes in this book. This struck me as somewhat odd—not that I didn't have scenes per se, but rather that someone without any scenes would be tapped to introduce. Then I realized that the production of the book had been so poorly managed that none of the main cast members had *time* to write an introduction. Due to the nature of the material, every one of the core six characters has at least one scene that's basically just them, and they were all swamped learning lines and such. The producers were essentially stuck using someone from the supporting cast, which, I can assure you, was terribly validating. I mean, nothing boosts the old ego like knowing the job was a toss up between you and one of the flumphs. Of course, it's somewhat worse to then find yourself accepting the job anyway. I really need to start feeling out new career options for myself one of these days.

The book you are holding in your hands is entitled *On the Origin of PCs*. (Say it out loud if you don't get the "joke", though I use that term loosely. Dreadful.) Again, this makes me an odd choice to lead the discussion, as I am not a PC. For those unfamiliar with the term, "PC" in gaming circles means "Player Character," the characters that are created and controlled by the players of a fantasy roleplaying game. They are the protagonists, and the world quite literally revolves around them. Incidentally, this makes them simply delightful to work with. I guess they're so used to appropriately-leveled encounters dropping in their lap that they get a bit testy when their bottle of spring water is the wrong brand.

But as I mentioned, I am not a PC, so I cannot comment on their respective trials and tribulations. I am, in fact, an NPC—or "Non-Player Character". Tremendously flattering terminology, isn't it? Apparently, someone felt I was to be defined solely by my innate lack of a player. They could have called us Gamemaster Characters, or Antagonist Characters, or maybe even Don't-Get-Snippy-When-the-Universe-Doesn't-Bend-to-Suit-Our-Petty-Needs Characters, though DGSWTUDBTSOPNCs doesn't exactly roll off the tongue.

Frankly, I've never thought not having a player has ever negatively impacted my life. I mean, I don't sit around listlessly wishing on a star that someone would play me. Heck, as far as I'm concerned, the presence of players is a necessary evil at best. I think most gamemasters will agree that their world functions significantly more smoothly before the PCs ever show up.

So what is it like to be an NPC? Well, it's a lot of waiting around, mostly. There's not a lot to do on set when you're waiting for the PCs to deign to appear in your dungeon corridor. You hang out, do the crossword, talk about last night's episode of *Lost*, that sort of thing. I like to bring the *New York Times*, personally, while my costar in the darkness tends to prefer the *Weekly World News*. Depending for whom you're working, the craft services table is sometimes pretty good. And then, of course, once the PCs show up, they need you to hit your mark and deliver your line right the first time, because the gods forbid any of the little prima donnas should have to do a second take.

I should also mention that as far as NPCs go, I'm one of the lucky ones. I've had a name since OOTS #95, which is more than I can say for most. Before that, I was just another goblin in a long line of disposable goblins. For a moment, imagine the inconvenience of going through life as Goblin #341. You can't vote, you can't get a driver's license, and your letters are always ending up in Goblin #314's mailbox, which is awkward because you used to date his cousin, Goblin #784, but it didn't work out because she needed to "find out who she really is", whatever that means. I'm sorry, but your stats are right in the *Monster Manual*. Crack the spine and end the mystery.

Oh, and lest I forget, the purpose of something like 80% of all NPCs is to get killed. It's kind of like wearing a red shirt on *Star Trek*, only instead of being killed to show that the main characters are in danger, you are actually executed *by* the main characters. It frankly disgusts me. But there's no shortage of young monsters with stars in their eyes, looking to make a name for themselves (literally) in the Next Big Dungeon. I blame the DMs, really, who take advantage of their naiveté with promises of recurring villain status and then instead send them off to get ground into hamburger by the PCs, just like every other random encounter.

I'm telling you, you don't know half of what goes on behind the scenes of these games. Don't even get me started on the recruitment policies. What the talent scouts will go through to sign a young dragon is downright criminal. Where do you think those dragon hoards come from, anyway? Someday, someone is going to write it all down and blow the lid off of the NPC industry.

Just you wait and see.

Redcloak
Goblin cleric
August 2005

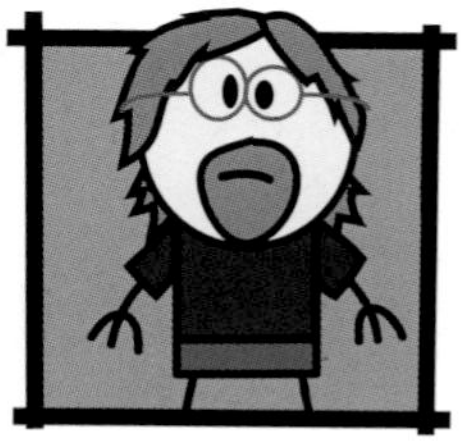

Introduction by Rich Burlew

OK, let's get this out of the way first: Yes, this is the second *Order of the Stick* book. No, it does not take place after the events of the first book, *The Order of the Stick: Dungeon Crawlin' Fools*. In fact, all of the events depicted in this volume take place BEFORE Roy and Elan and the gang arrive in the Redmountain Hills, as seen at the start of that first book. That makes this (drum roll, please)...a prequel! Yeah, George Lucas, eat your heart out.

Even though this book is chronologically earlier than *Dungeon Crawlin' Fools*, I strongly recommend you read that book first. Why? Well, because many of the stories in here will give away things that happen in those strips. They were written first, so the concepts there were often introduced better. In fact, I would go so far as to say you should read all of the strips online at **www.GiantITP.com** before reading this prequel (or read the forthcoming third book, which will compile them). For example, I already assume the reader knows what is written in the letter Haley gets from Tyrinaria—information not revealed until *OOTS* #131 of the main strip.

So consider the content in this book supplemental material for the main (color) comic strip. In these pages, you'll find out a little more about the OOTSers, who they were before they met each other, how they met, and what kind of people they are. While I like to think it's still plenty funny, I didn't stick to a strict one-punchline-a-page format. Because it is all-new material, I was able run a scene continuously over several pages, which was a major change for my *OOTS* writing style. And the fact that it is "all-new" bears mentioning, too; this is the first *OOTS* book that is entirely fashioned from comics that never have been online and never *will be* online. That was the main reason I chose to make it a prequel rather than a part of the ongoing story; not everyone is going to have the means to buy this book, and I didn't want anyone missing out on key plot elements because of that.

Which is not to imply that the events in this book "didn't happen", or will not impact the characters and plots of the main strip. Quite the opposite. It's just that should readers of the main strip ever NEED to know something contained in these backstories, it will probably just be summarized in the strip in question. Whereas you, gentle reader, can relive the scenes in excruciating panel-by-panel detail, reveling in their grey-hued glory.

Which brings up a good point, oddly. You may be wondering why on earth this book is in greyscale, when *OOTS* has always been in glorious full color. Clearly, it is to give it that "nostalgic" feeling, so that you really feel like you are peering into the past. After all, these are the "home movies" of the *OOTS* characters, and so black-and-white seemed appropriate. I was outraged to learn that it was, in fact, less expensive and faster to produce, and insisted on paying the printer the full cost for a color book, simply to appease my conscience. That's just the kind of guy I am.

After reading the book, you might wonder why some of the characters have detailed origins that explain everything about them, while others simply have scenes that predate their appearance on Roy's team by a few days. Well, there are two answers: the roleplaying answer and the writing answer. The roleplaying answer is that in any gaming group, there is the guy that writes 34 pages of background information for his 1st level fighter, and then there is the guy who writes nothing for a character starting at 15th level. Every player has a different idea of how much backstory is appropriate or even desirable. While I usually err on the side of too much background, I've run characters whose entire history could be summed up by one sentence. I thought the OOTSers should reflect that same sort of diversity in their character histories.

The writing answer is that some characters demand a backstory to explain why they act the way they do, and others would be ruined by it. Do we really want to know why Belkar is so psychotic? For example, if I created a backstory where Belkar was emotionally scarred as a child, wouldn't his outrageous behavior become more sad than funny? In a similar vein, some people were upset when I revealed the "reason" behind Haley's cash hoarding, though hopefully her history in this book will set straight that she was a greedy thief long before she ever had to raise 200,000 gp to save her dad from the dungeons of Tyrinaria. (Hey, I guess now you know what the letter said, too. Never mind, then.) And in at least one case, I wasn't ready to reveal a history that will, in part, be integral to the main plot of *Order of the Stick*, so I chose a different scene from that character's previous life.

OK, I see the end of the page coming up, so my rambling is officially done for this book. Be glad this isn't a compilation, or else you'd have like ten more pages of this to deal with. You got off easy this time, punk.

Rich Burlew
July 2005

Haley Starshine

Human rogue
8 months ago

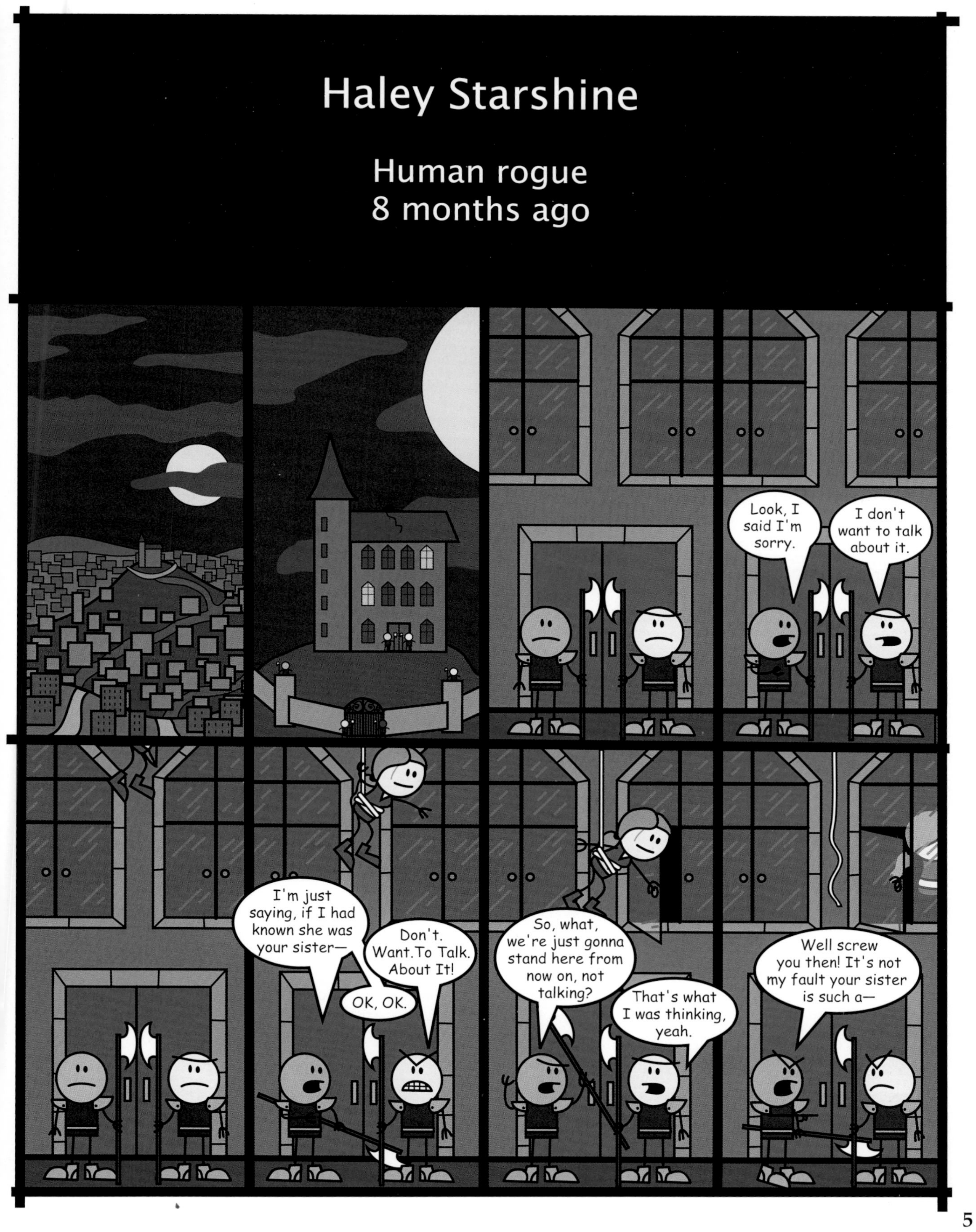

Look, I said I'm sorry.
I don't want to talk about it.
I'm just saying, if I had known she was your sister—
Don't. Want.To Talk. About It!
OK, OK.
So, what, we're just gonna stand here from now on, not talking?
That's what I was thinking, yeah.
Well screw you then! It's not my fault your sister is such a—

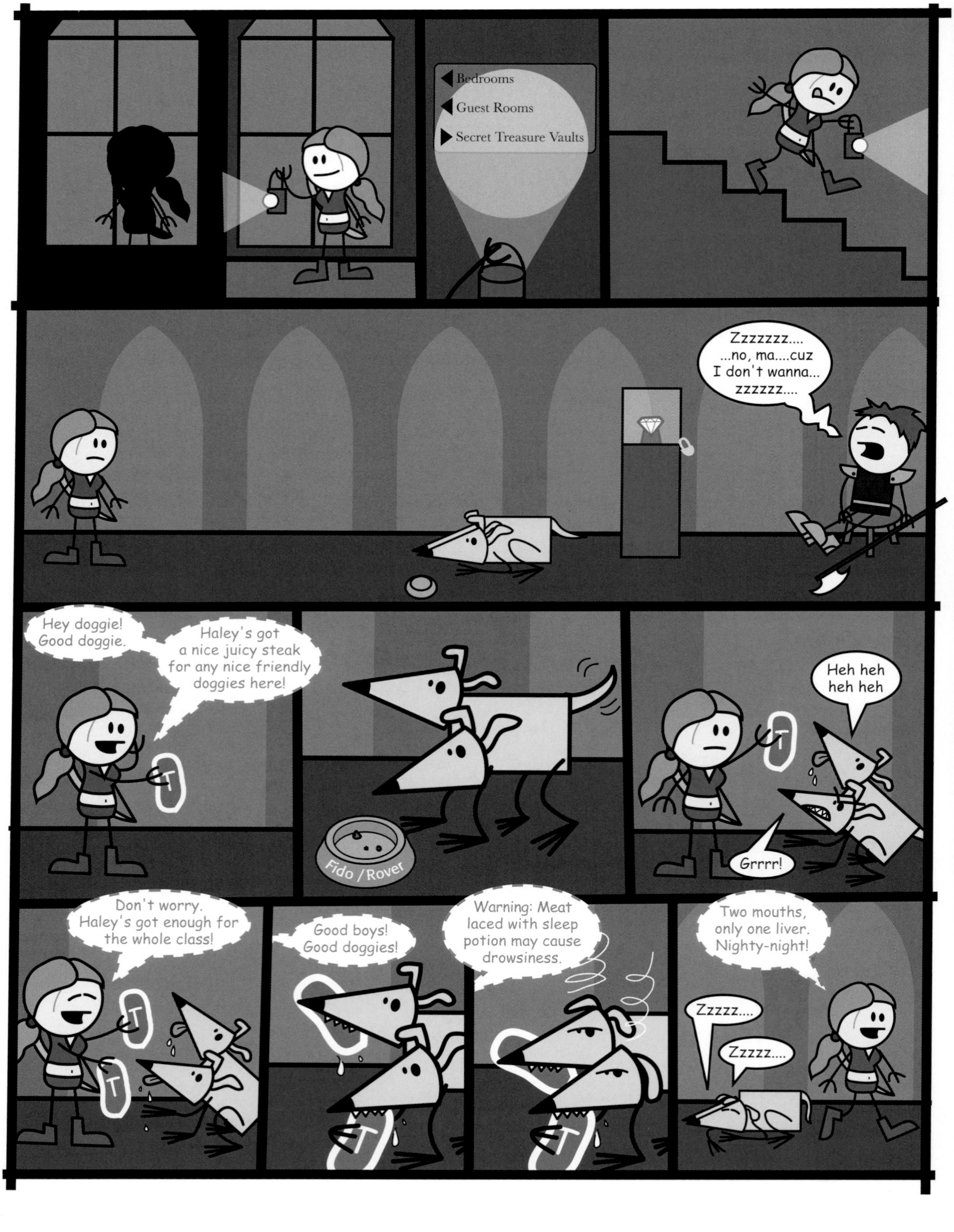
Bedrooms
Guest Rooms
Secret Treasure Vaults
Zzzzzzz.... ...no, ma....cuz I don't wanna... zzzzzz....
Hey doggie! Good doggie.
Haley's got a nice juicy steak for any nice friendly doggies here!
Fido / Rover
Heh heh heh heh
Grrrr!
Don't worry. Haley's got enough for the whole class!
Good boys! Good doggies!
Warning: Meat laced with sleep potion may cause drowsiness.
Two mouths, only one liver. Nighty-night!
Zzzzz....
Zzzzz....

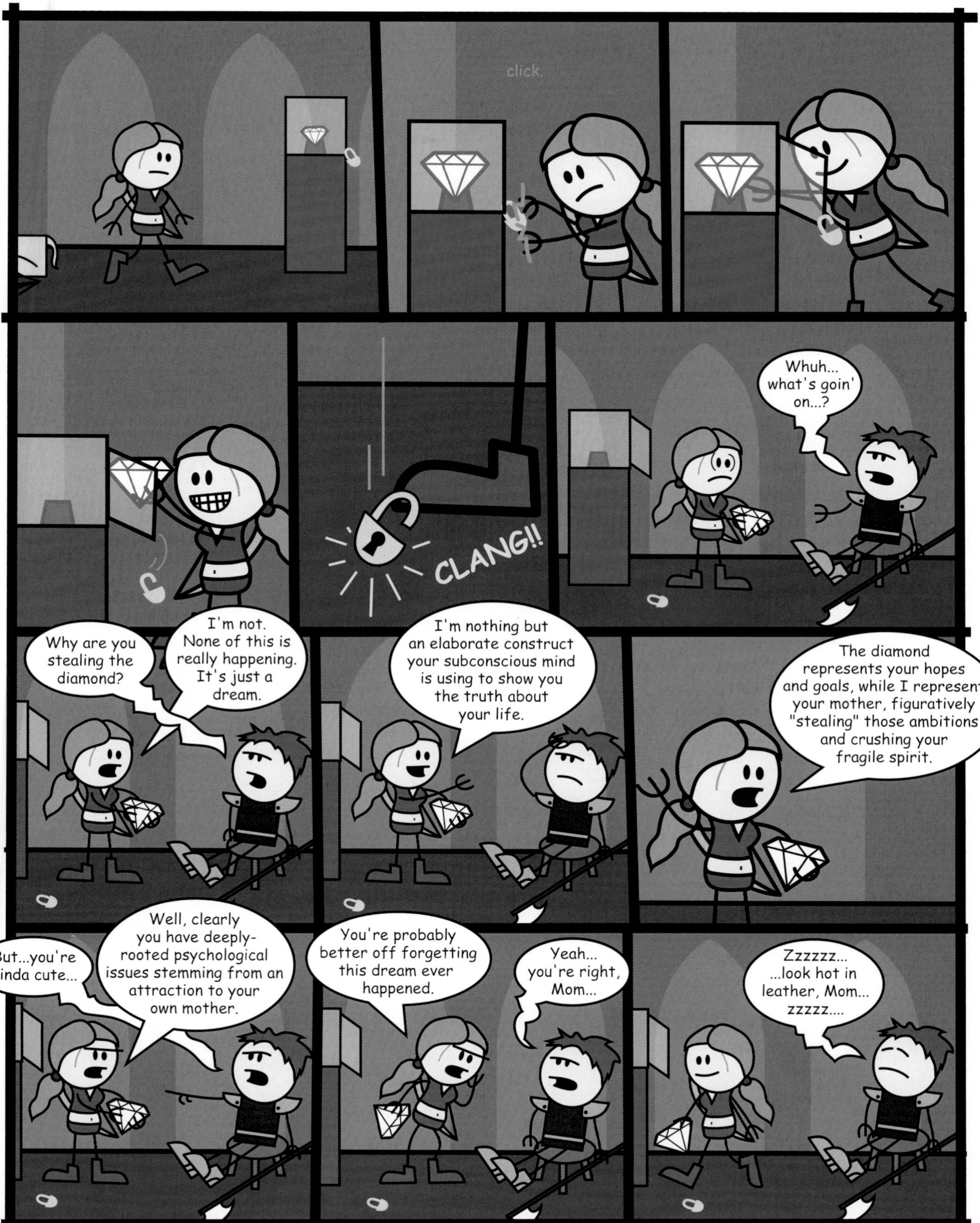
click.
CLANG!!
Whuh... what's goin' on...?
Why are you stealing the diamond?
I'm not. None of this is really happening. It's just a dream.
I'm nothing but an elaborate construct your subconscious mind is using to show you the truth about your life.
The diamond represents your hopes and goals, while I represent your mother, figuratively "stealing" those ambitions and crushing your fragile spirit.
But...you're kinda cute...
Well, clearly you have deeply-rooted psychological issues stemming from an attraction to your own mother.
You're probably better off forgetting this dream ever happened.
Yeah... you're right, Mom...
Zzzzzz... ...look hot in leather, Mom... zzzzz....

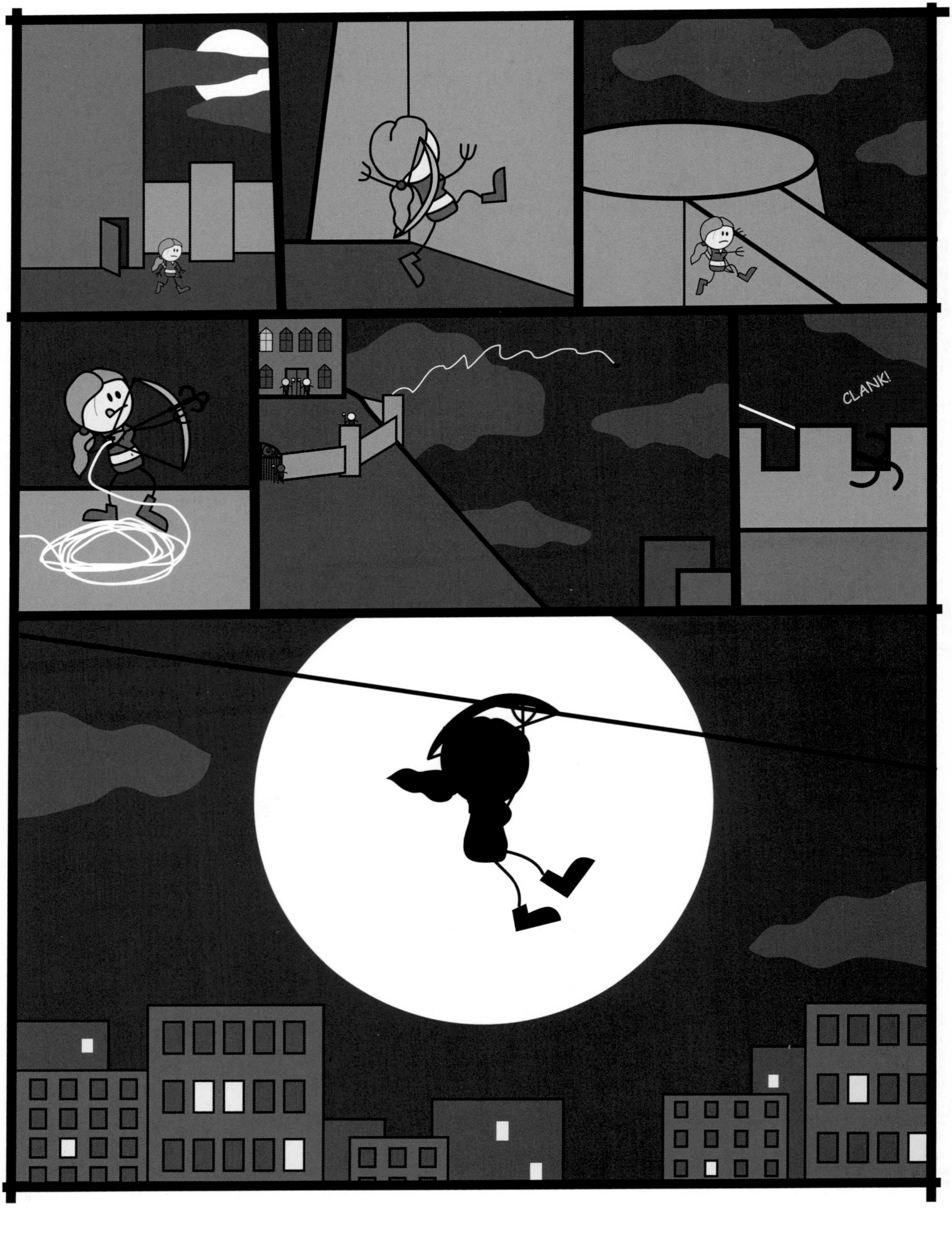
CLANK!

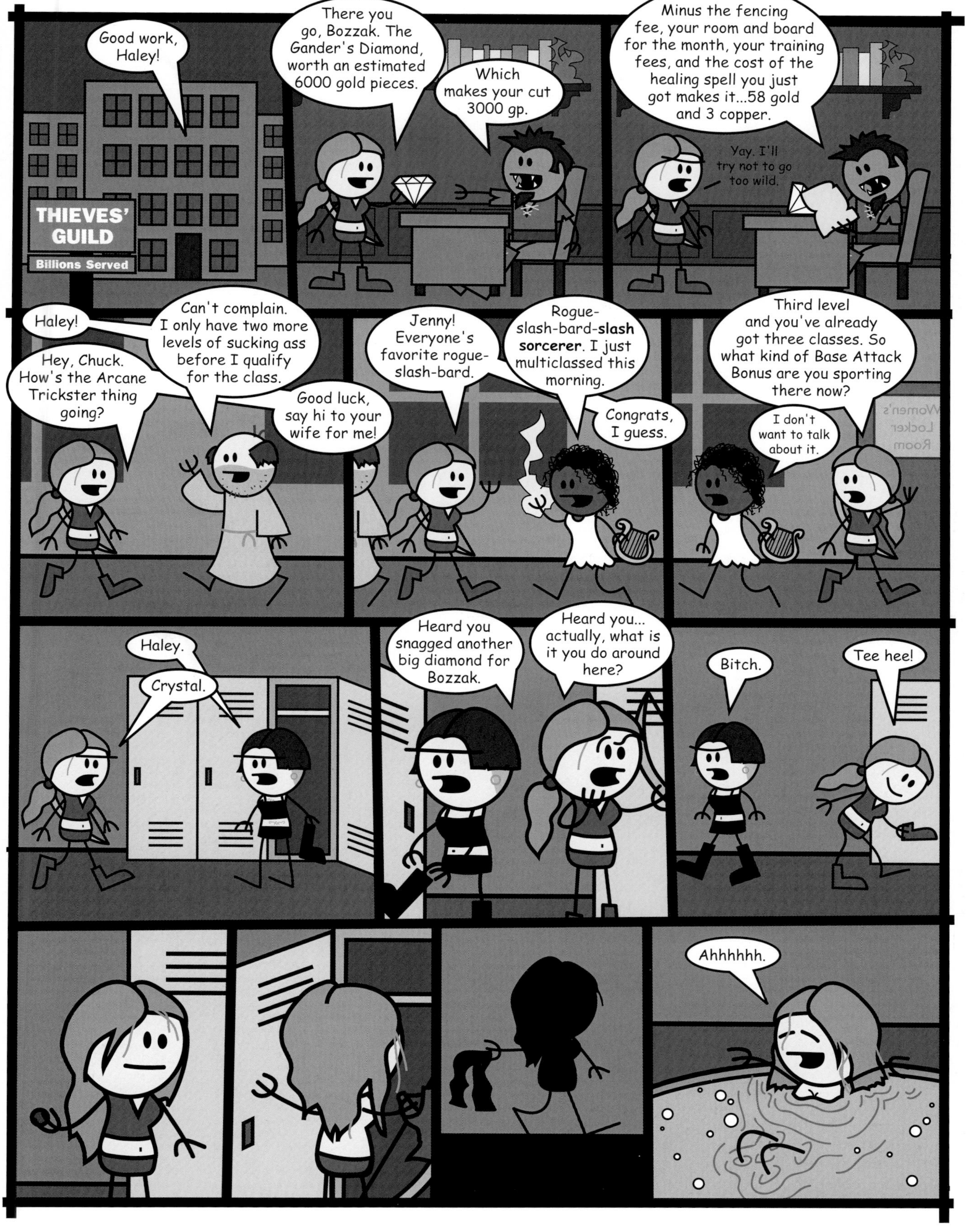
Good work, Haley!
THIEVES' GUILD
Billions Served
There you go, Bozzak. The Gander's Diamond, worth an estimated 6000 gold pieces.
Which makes your cut 3000 gp.
Minus the fencing fee, your room and board for the month, your training fees, and the cost of the healing spell you just got makes it...58 gold and 3 copper.
Yay. I'll try not to go too wild.
Haley!
Hey, Chuck. How's the Arcane Trickster thing going?
Can't complain. I only have two more levels of sucking ass before I qualify for the class.
Good luck, say hi to your wife for me!
Jenny! Everyone's favorite rogue-slash-bard.
Rogue-slash-bard-**slash sorcerer**. I just multiclassed this morning.
Congrats, I guess.
Third level and you've already got three classes. So what kind of Base Attack Bonus are you sporting there now?
I don't want to talk about it.
Women's Locker Room
Haley.
Crystal.
Heard you snagged another big diamond for Bozzak.
Heard you... actually, what is it you do around here?
Bitch.
Tee hee!
Ahhhhhh.

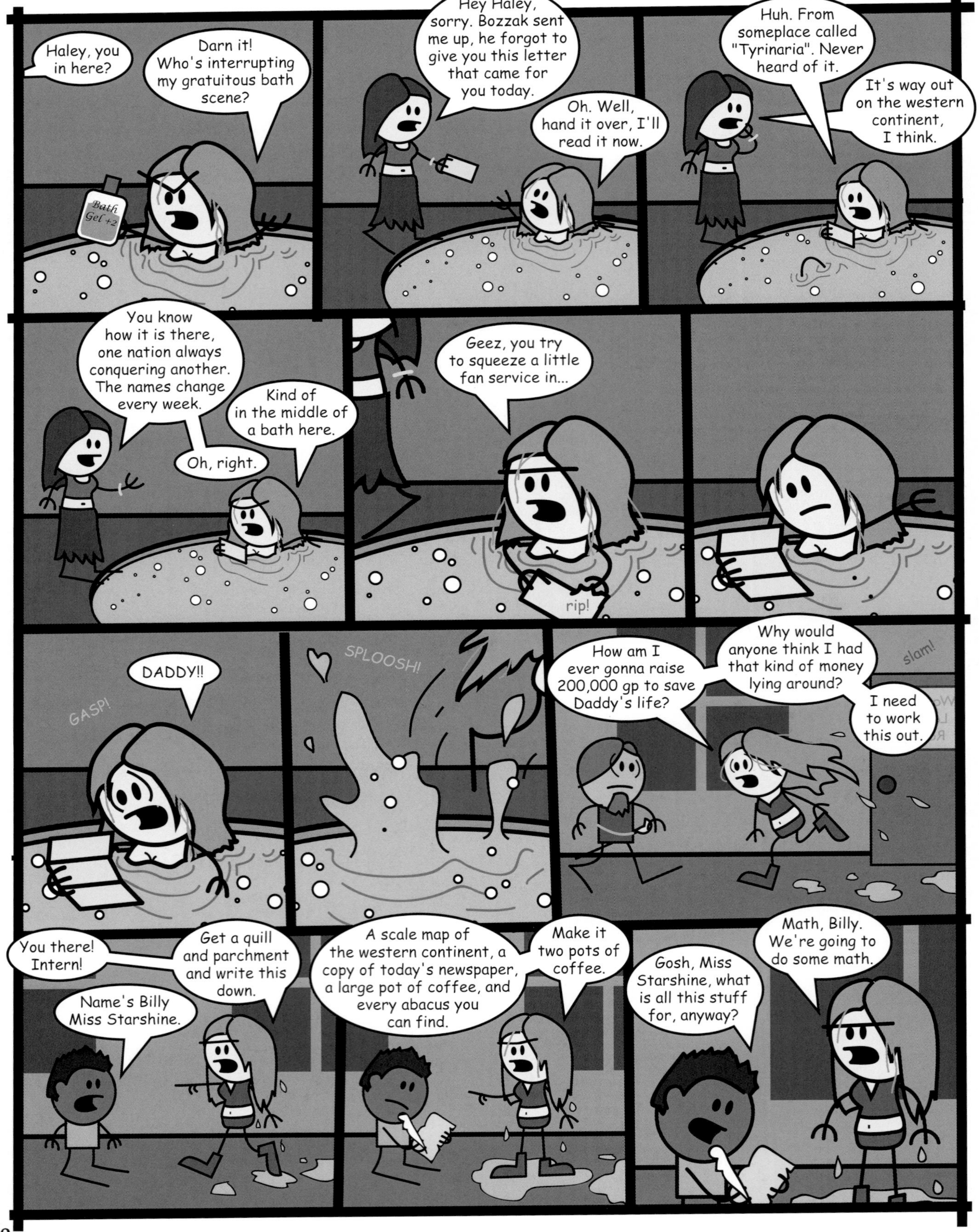
Haley, you in here?
Darn it! Who's interrupting my gratuitous bath scene?
Bath Gel +2
Hey Haley, sorry. Bozzak sent me up, he forgot to give you this letter that came for you today.
Oh. Well, hand it over, I'll read it now.
Huh. From someplace called "Tyrinaria". Never heard of it.
It's way out on the western continent, I think.
You know how it is there, one nation always conquering another. The names change every week.
Oh, right.
Kind of in the middle of a bath here.
Geez, you try to squeeze a little fan service in...
rip!
DADDY!!
GASP!
SPLOOSH!
How am I ever gonna raise 200,000 gp to save Daddy's life?
Why would anyone think I had that kind of money lying around?
I need to work this out.
slam!
You there! Intern!
Get a quill and parchment and write this down.
Name's Billy Miss Starshine.
A scale map of the western continent, a copy of today's newspaper, a large pot of coffee, and every abacus you can find.
Make it two pots of coffee.
Gosh, Miss Starshine, what is all this stuff for, anyway?
Math, Billy. We're going to do some math.

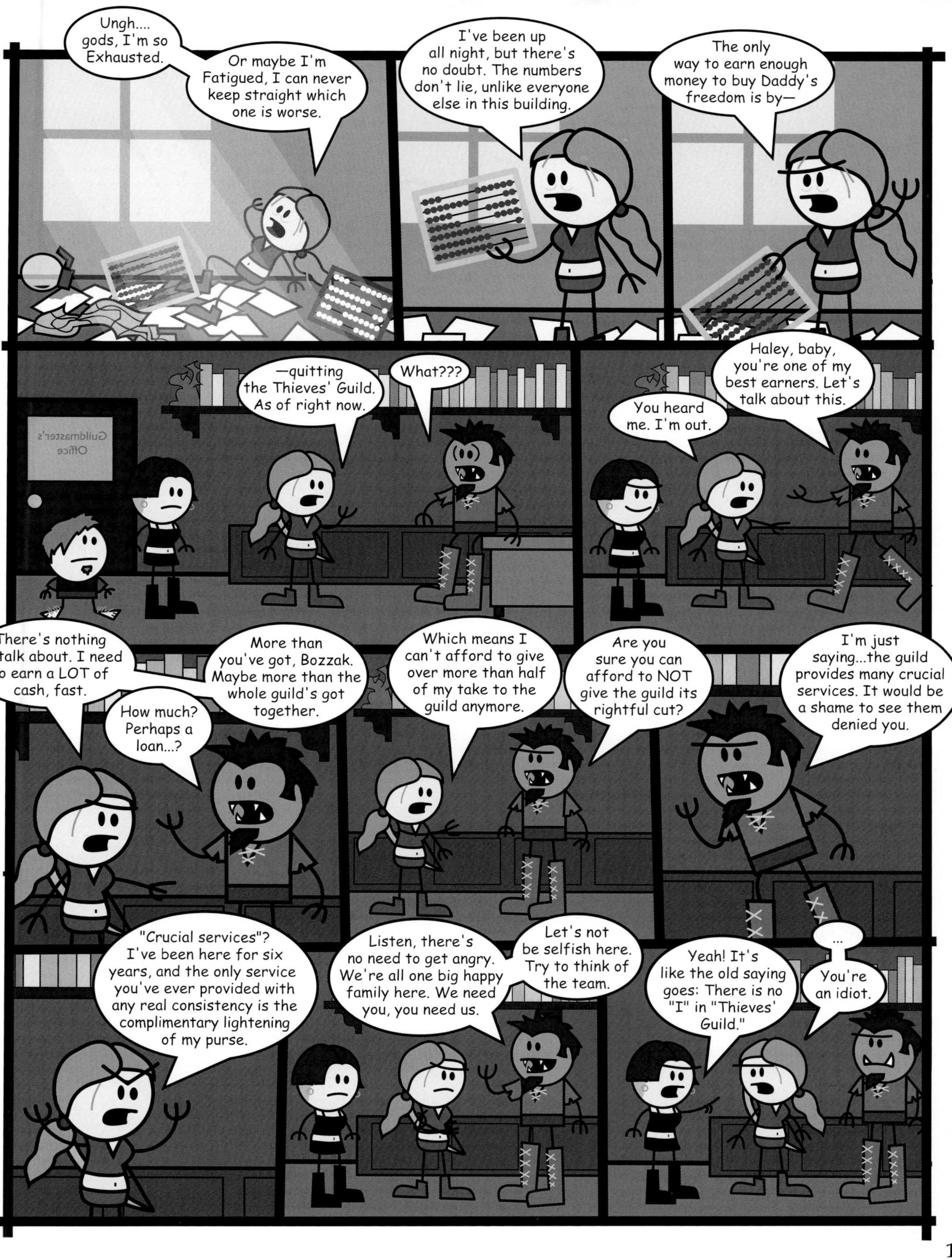

Ungh.... gods, I'm so Exhausted.
Or maybe I'm Fatigued, I can never keep straight which one is worse.
I've been up all night, but there's no doubt. The numbers don't lie, unlike everyone else in this building.
The only way to earn enough money to buy Daddy's freedom is by—
Guildmaster's Office
—quitting the Thieves' Guild. As of right now.
What???
You heard me. I'm out.
Haley, baby, you're one of my best earners. Let's talk about this.
There's nothing o talk about. I need to earn a LOT of cash, fast.
How much? Perhaps a loan...?
More than you've got, Bozzak. Maybe more than the whole guild's got together.
Which means I can't afford to give over more than half of my take to the guild anymore.
Are you sure you can afford to NOT give the guild its rightful cut?
I'm just saying...the guild provides many crucial services. It would be a shame to see them denied you.
"Crucial services"? I've been here for six years, and the only service you've ever provided with any real consistency is the complimentary lightening of my purse.
Listen, there's no need to get angry. We're all one big happy family here. We need you, you need us.
Let's not be selfish here. Try to think of the team.
Yeah! It's like the old saying goes: There is no "I" in "Thieves' Guild."
...
You're an idiot.

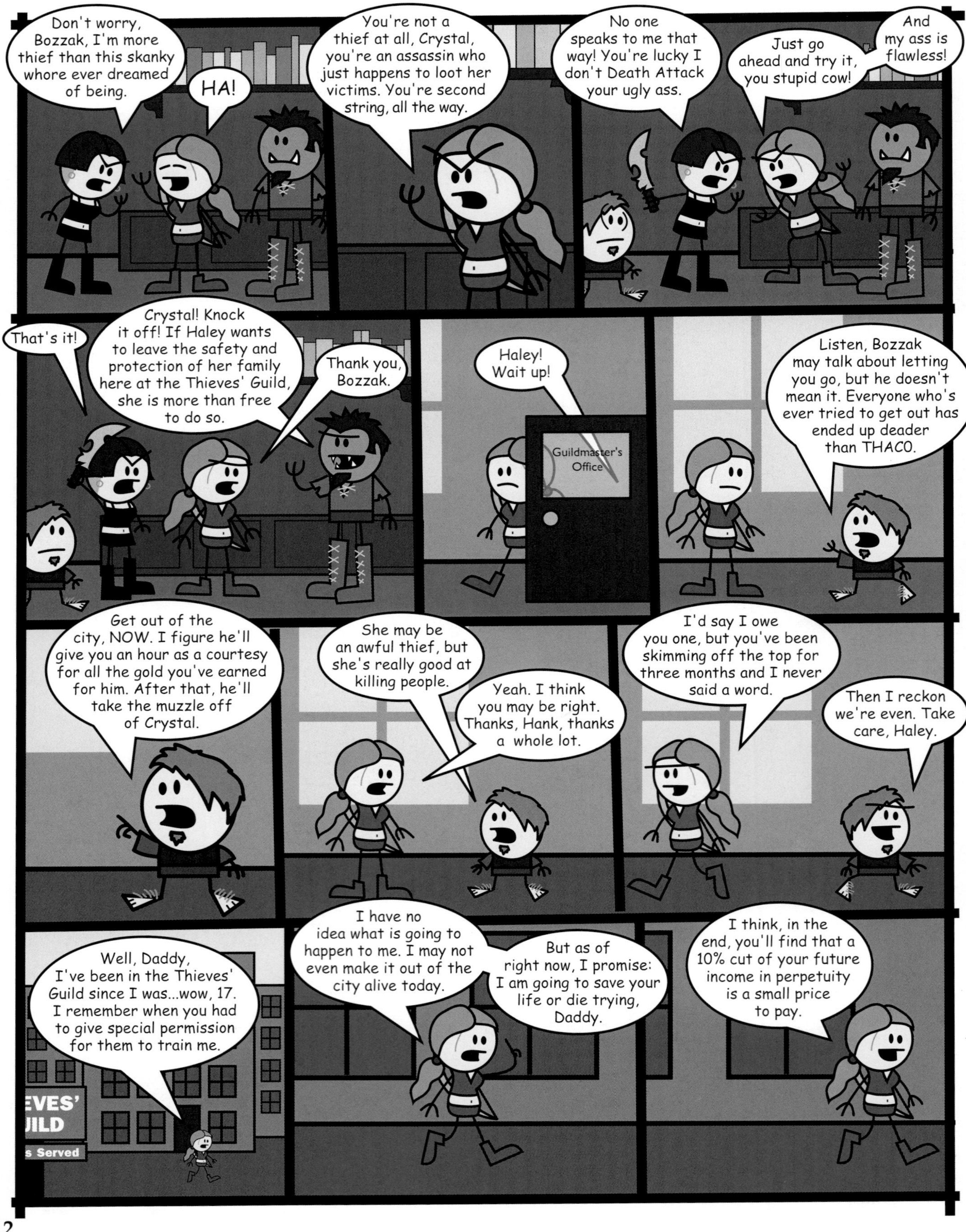
Don't worry, Bozzak, I'm more thief than this skanky whore ever dreamed of being.
HA!
You're not a thief at all, Crystal, you're an assassin who just happens to loot her victims. You're second string, all the way.
No one speaks to me that way! You're lucky I don't Death Attack your ugly ass.
Just go ahead and try it, you stupid cow!
And my ass is flawless!
That's it!
Crystal! Knock it off! If Haley wants to leave the safety and protection of her family here at the Thieves' Guild, she is more than free to do so.
Thank you, Bozzak.
Haley! Wait up!
Guildmaster's Office
Listen, Bozzak may talk about letting you go, but he doesn't mean it. Everyone who's ever tried to get out has ended up deader than THAC0.
Get out of the city, NOW. I figure he'll give you an hour as a courtesy for all the gold you've earned for him. After that, he'll take the muzzle off of Crystal.
She may be an awful thief, but she's really good at killing people.
Yeah. I think you may be right. Thanks, Hank, thanks a whole lot.
I'd say I owe you one, but you've been skimming off the top for three months and I never said a word.
Then I reckon we're even. Take care, Haley.
Well, Daddy, I've been in the Thieves' Guild since I was...wow, 17. I remember when you had to give special permission for them to train me.
EVES'
UILD
s Served
I have no idea what is going to happen to me. I may not even make it out of the city alive today.
But as of right now, I promise: I am going to save your life or die trying, Daddy.
I think, in the end, you'll find that a 10% cut of your future income in perpetuity is a small price to pay.

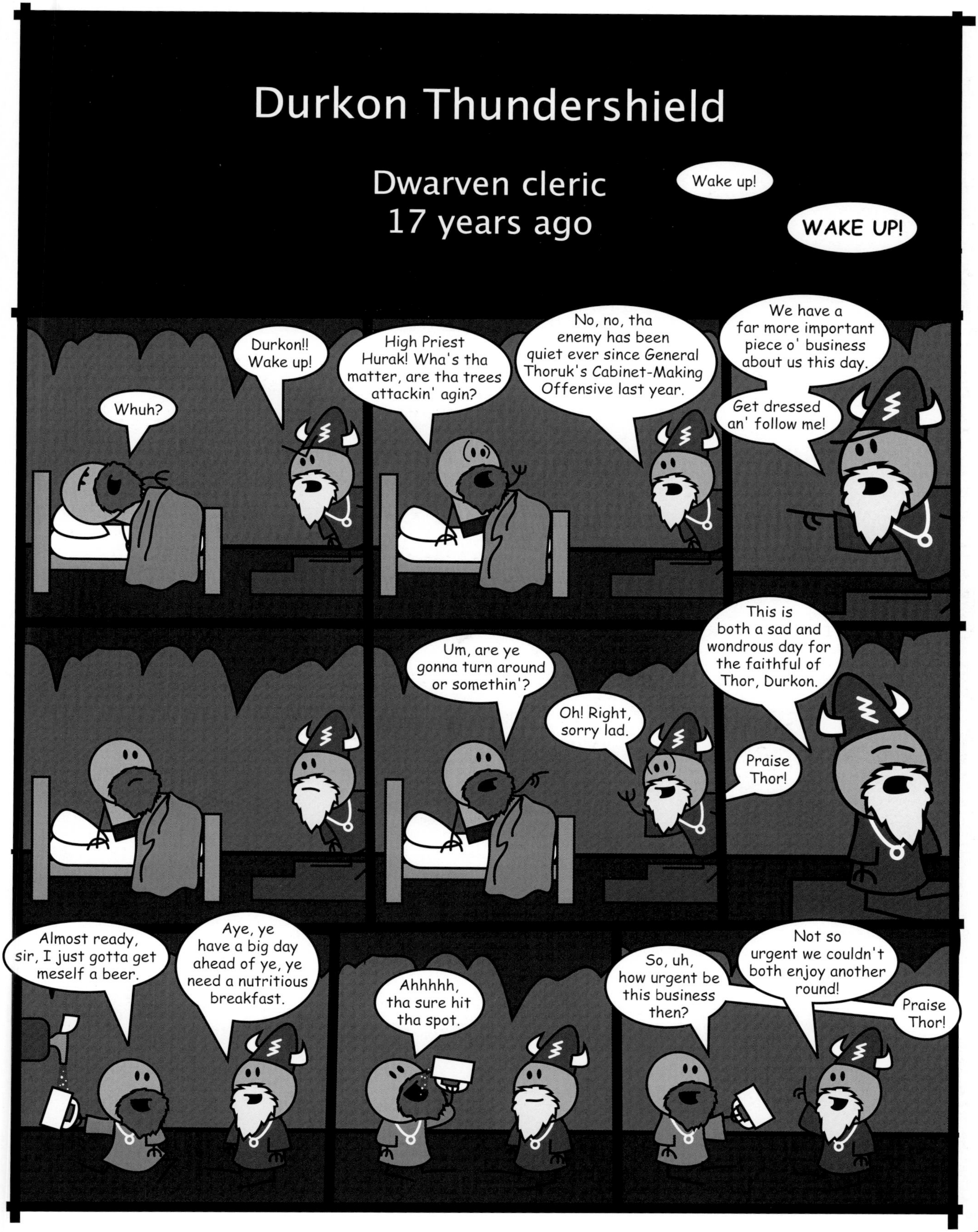
Durkon Thundershield
Dwarven cleric
17 years ago
Wake up!
WAKE UP!
Whuh?
Durkon!! Wake up!
High Priest Hurak! Wha's tha matter, are tha trees attackin' agin?
No, no, tha enemy has been quiet ever since General Thoruk's Cabinet-Making Offensive last year.
We have a far more important piece o' business about us this day.
Get dressed an' follow me!
Um, are ye gonna turn around or somethin'?
Oh! Right, sorry lad.
This is both a sad and wondrous day for the faithful of Thor, Durkon.
Praise Thor!
Almost ready, sir, I just gotta get meself a beer.
Aye, ye have a big day ahead of ye, ye need a nutritious breakfast.
Ahhhhh, tha sure hit tha spot.
So, uh, how urgent be this business then?
Not so urgent we couldn't both enjoy another round!
Praise Thor!

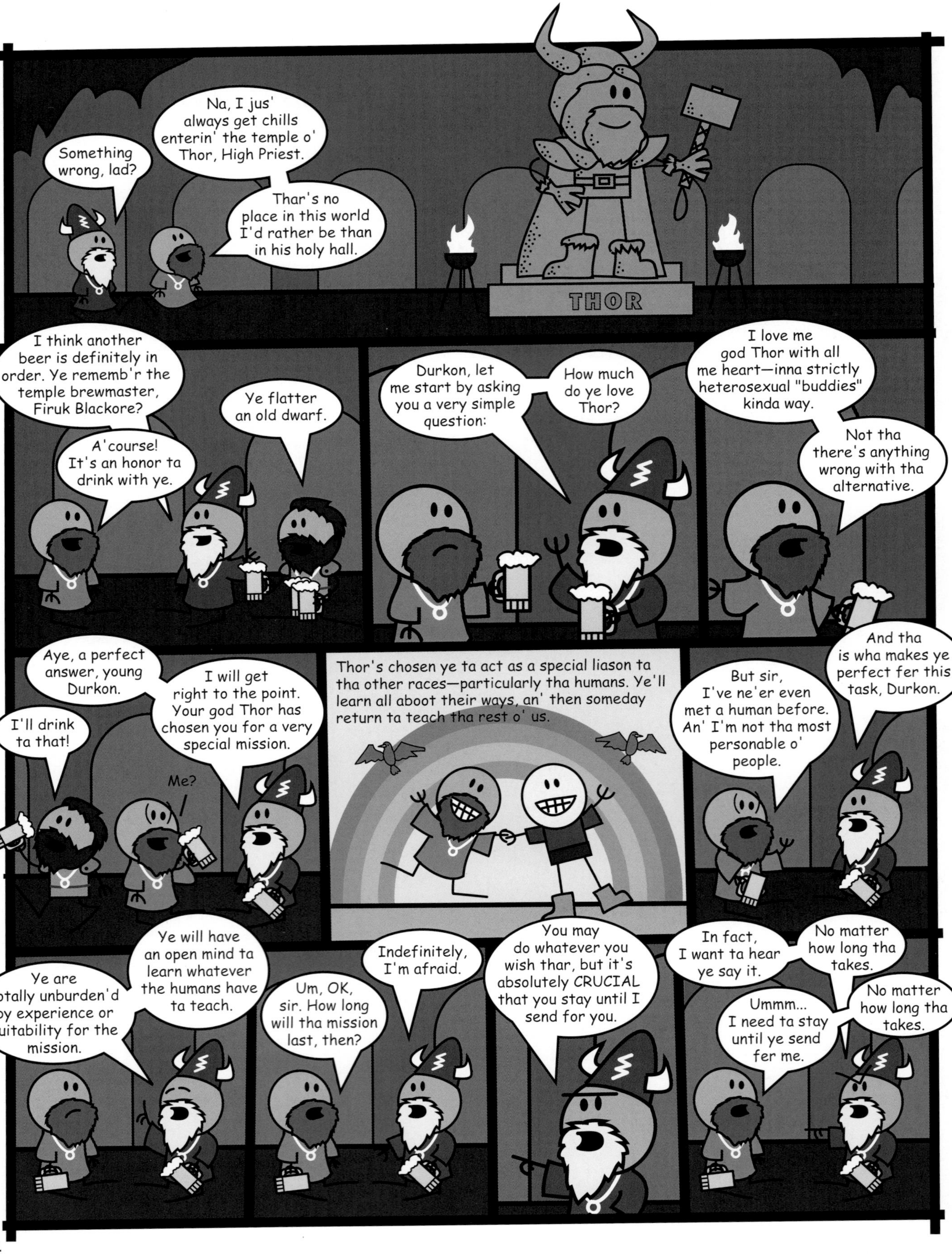
Something wrong, lad?
Na, I jus' always get chills enterin' the temple o' Thor, High Priest.
Thar's no place in this world I'd rather be than in his holy hall.
THOR
I think another beer is definitely in order. Ye rememb'r the temple brewmaster, Firuk Blackore?
A'course! It's an honor ta drink with ye.
Ye flatter an old dwarf.
Durkon, let me start by asking you a very simple question:
How much do ye love Thor?
I love me god Thor with all me heart—inna strictly heterosexual "buddies" kinda way.
Not tha there's anything wrong with tha alternative.
Aye, a perfect answer, young Durkon.
I'll drink ta that!
I will get right to the point. Your god Thor has chosen you for a very special mission.
Me?
Thor's chosen ye ta act as a special liason ta tha other races—particularly tha humans. Ye'll learn all aboot their ways, an' then someday return ta teach tha rest o' us.
But sir, I've ne'er even met a human before. An' I'm not tha most personable o' people.
And tha is wha makes ye perfect fer this task, Durkon.
Ye are totally unburden'd by experience or suitability for the mission.
Ye will have an open mind ta learn whatever the humans have ta teach.
Um, OK, sir. How long will tha mission last, then?
Indefinitely, I'm afraid.
You may do whatever you wish thar, but it's absolutely CRUCIAL that you stay until I send for you.
In fact, I want ta hear ye say it.
No matter how long tha takes.
Ummm... I need ta stay until ye send fer me.
No matter how long tha takes.

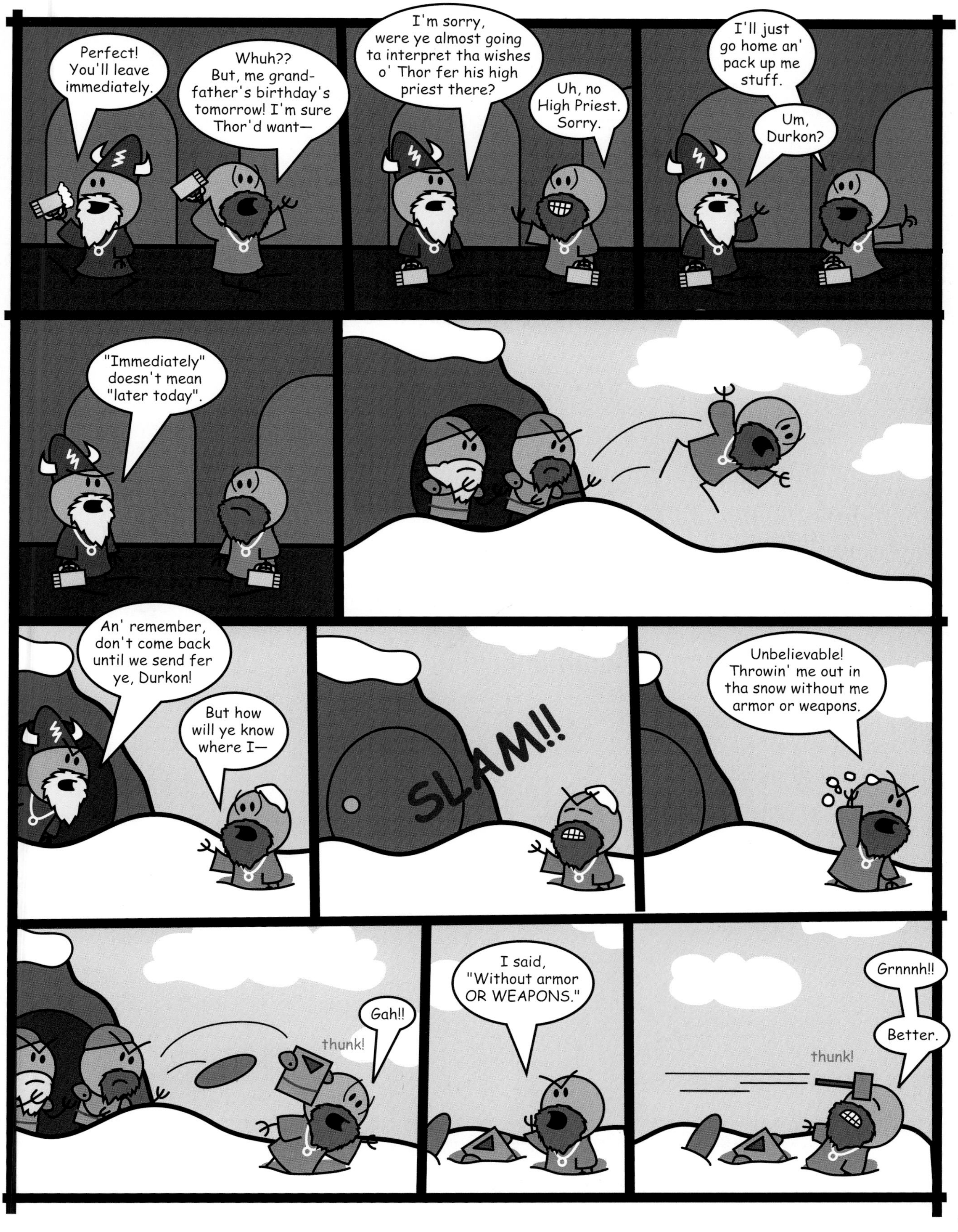
Perfect! You'll leave immediately.
Whuh?? But, me grand-father's birthday's tomorrow! I'm sure Thor'd want—
I'm sorry, were ye almost going ta interpret tha wishes o' Thor fer his high priest there?
Uh, no High Priest. Sorry.
I'll just go home an' pack up me stuff.
Um, Durkon?
"Immediately" doesn't mean "later today".
An' remember, don't come back until we send fer ye, Durkon!
But how will ye know where I—
SLAM!!
Unbelievable! Throwin' me out in tha snow without me armor or weapons.
thunk!
Gah!!
I said, "Without armor OR WEAPONS."
thunk!
Grnnnh!!
Better.

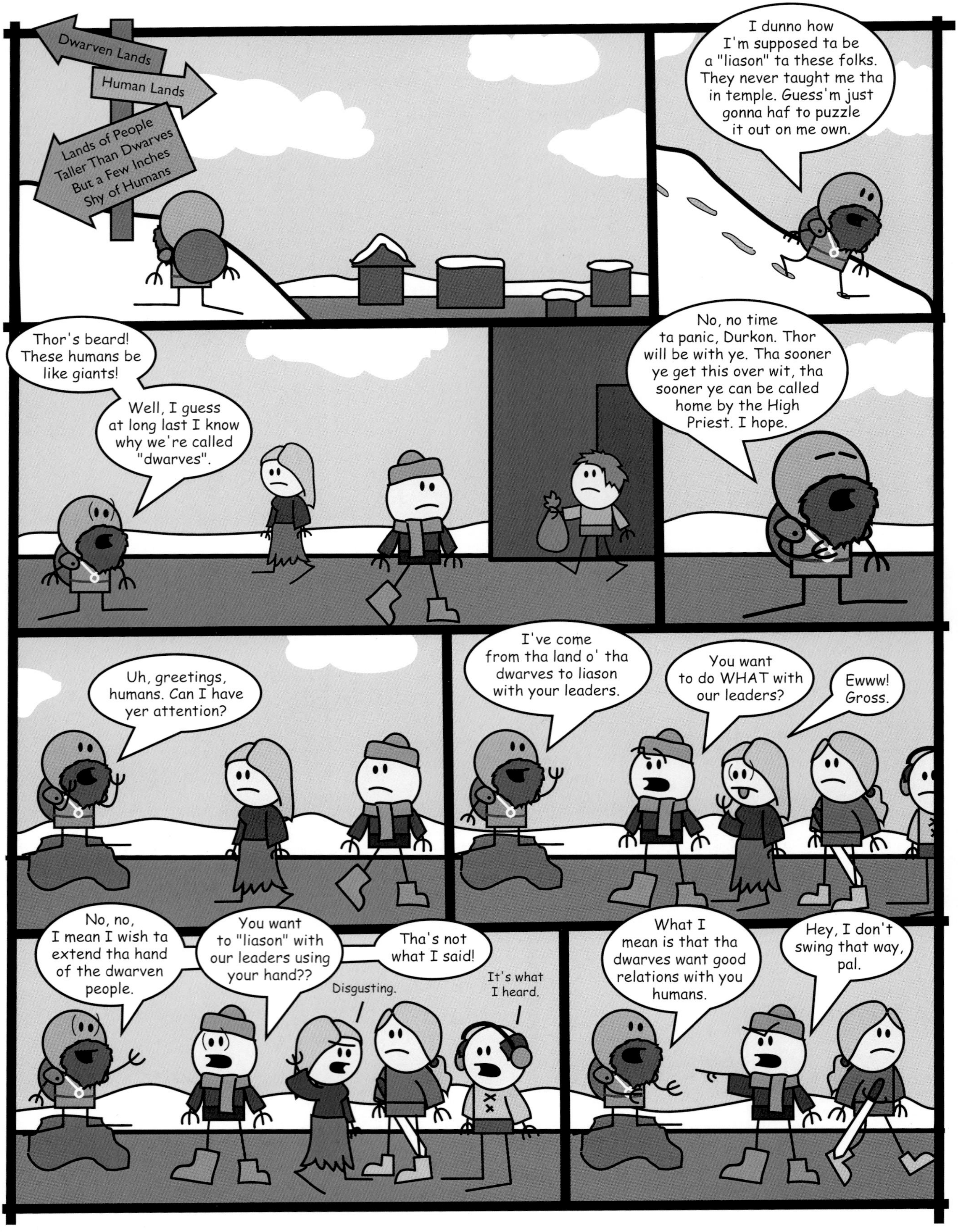
Dwarven Lands
Human Lands
Lands of People Taller Than Dwarves But a Few Inches Shy of Humans
I dunno how I'm supposed ta be a "liason" ta these folks. They never taught me tha in temple. Guess'm just gonna haf to puzzle it out on me own.
Thor's beard! These humans be like giants!
Well, I guess at long last I know why we're called "dwarves".
No, no time ta panic, Durkon. Thor will be with ye. Tha sooner ye get this over wit, tha sooner ye can be called home by the High Priest. I hope.
Uh, greetings, humans. Can I have yer attention?
I've come from tha land o' tha dwarves to liason with your leaders.
You want to do WHAT with our leaders?
Ewww! Gross.
No, no, I mean I wish ta extend tha hand of the dwarven people.
You want to "liason" with our leaders using your hand??
Tha's not what I said!
Disgusting.
It's what I heard.
What I mean is that tha dwarves want good relations with you humans.
Hey, I don't swing that way, pal.

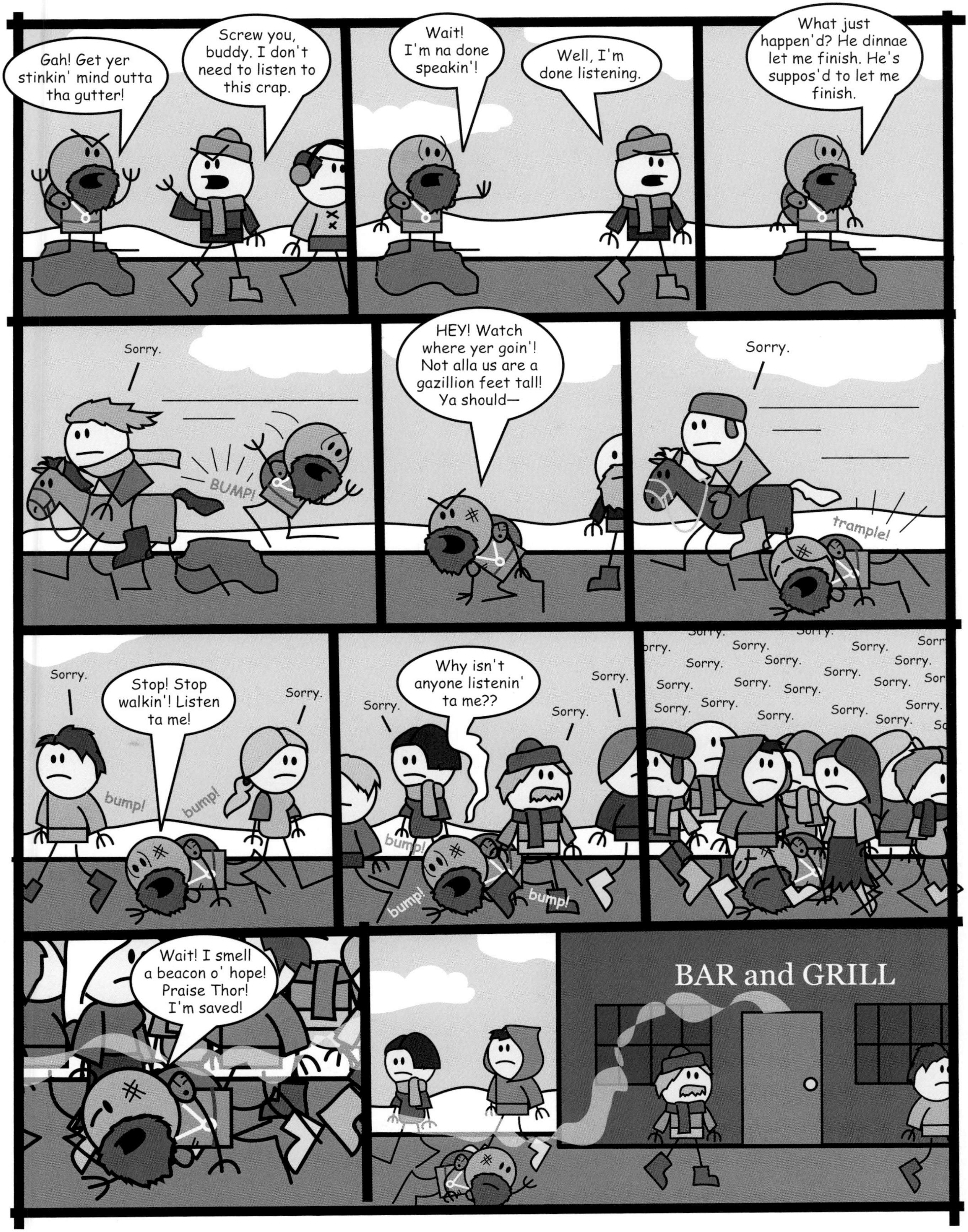

Gah! Get yer stinkin' mind outta tha gutter!
Screw you, buddy. I don't need to listen to this crap.
Wait! I'm na done speakin'!
Well, I'm done listening.
What just happen'd? He dinnae let me finish. He's suppos'd to let me finish.
Sorry.
BUMP!
HEY! Watch where yer goin'! Not alla us are a gazillion feet tall! Ya should—
Sorry.
trample!
Sorry.
Stop! Stop walkin'! Listen ta me!
Sorry.
bump!
bump!
Sorry.
Why isn't anyone listenin' ta me??
Sorry.
Sorry.
bump!
bump!
bump!
Sorry. Sorry. Sorry. Sorry. Sorry. Sorry. Sorry. Sorry. Sorry. Sorry. Sorry. Sorry. Sorry. Sorry. Sorry. Sorry. Sorry. Sorry.
Wait! I smell a beacon o' hope! Praise Thor! I'm saved!
BAR and GRILL

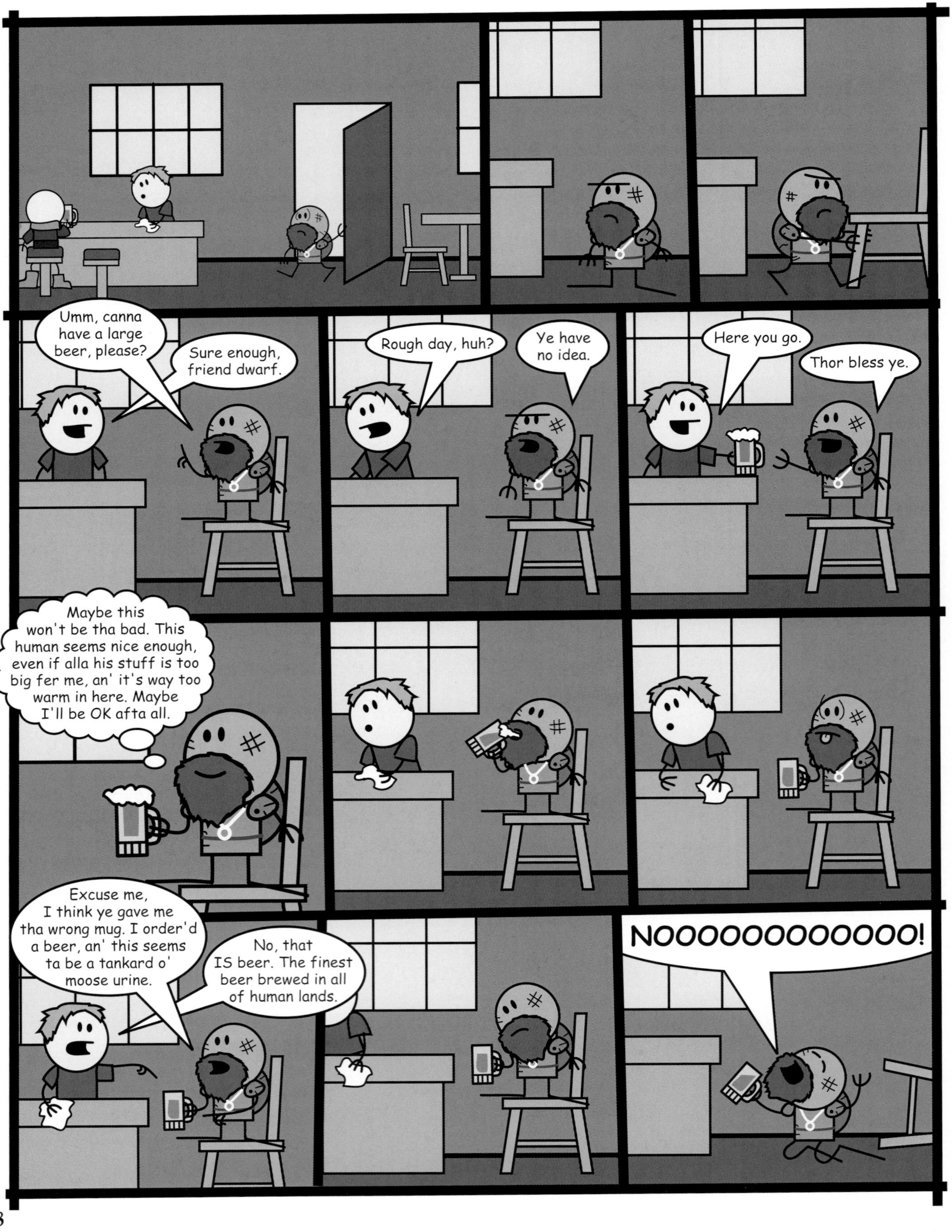

Umm, canna have a large beer, please?
Sure enough, friend dwarf.
Rough day, huh?
Ye have no idea.
Here you go.
Thor bless ye.
Maybe this won't be tha bad. This human seems nice enough, even if alla his stuff is too big fer me, an' it's way too warm in here. Maybe I'll be OK afta all.
Excuse me, I think ye gave me tha wrong mug. I order'd a beer, an' this seems ta be a tankard o' moose urine.
No, that IS beer. The finest beer brewed in all of human lands.
NOOOOOOOOOOOO!

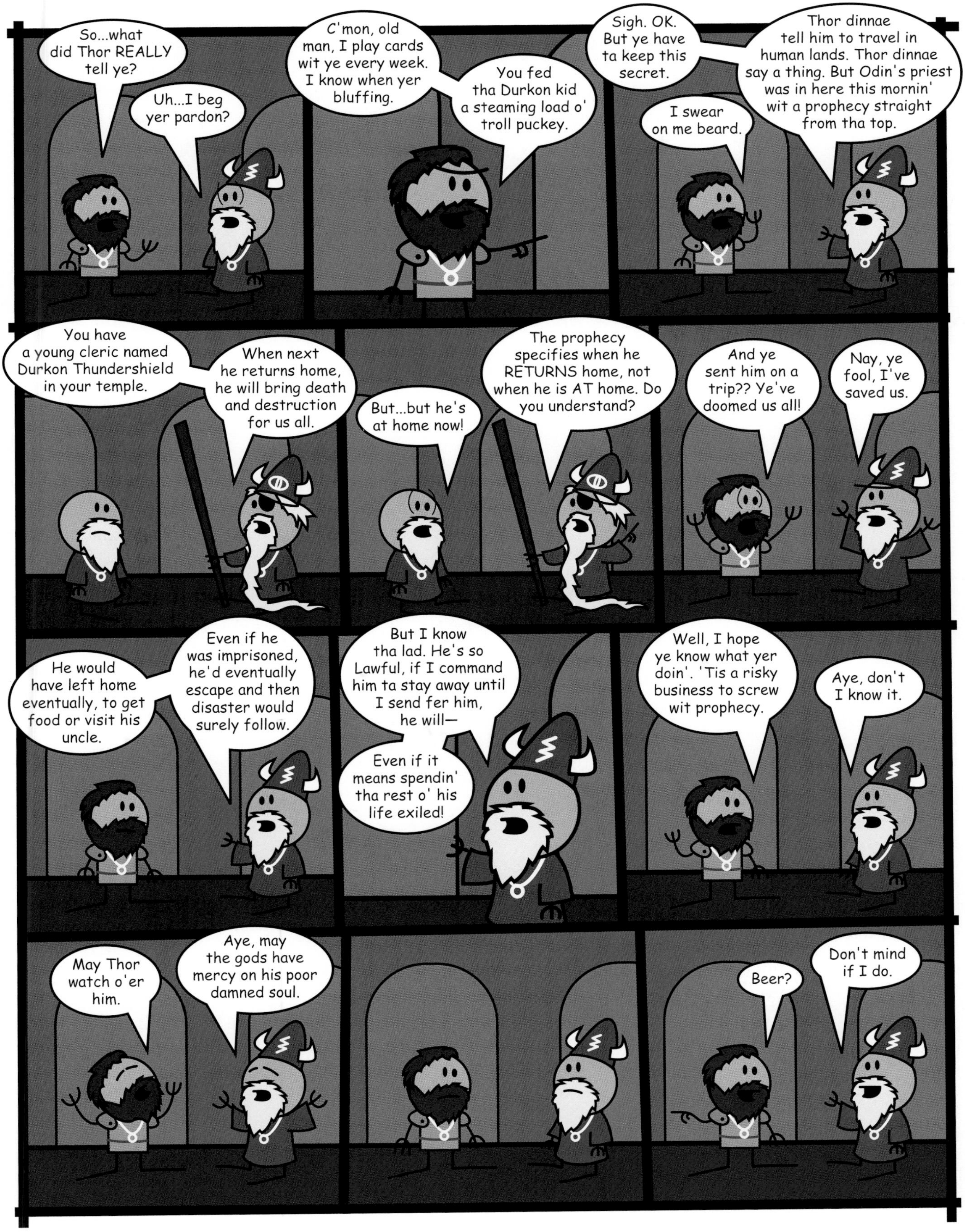

So...what did Thor REALLY tell ye?
Uh...I beg yer pardon?
C'mon, old man, I play cards wit ye every week. I know when yer bluffing.
You fed tha Durkon kid a steaming load o' troll puckey.
Sigh. OK. But ye have ta keep this secret.
I swear on me beard.
Thor dinnae tell him to travel in human lands. Thor dinnae say a thing. But Odin's priest was in here this mornin' wit a prophecy straight from tha top.
You have a young cleric named Durkon Thundershield in your temple.
When next he returns home, he will bring death and destruction for us all.
But...but he's at home now!
The prophecy specifies when he RETURNS home, not when he is AT home. Do you understand?
And ye sent him on a trip?? Ye've doomed us all!
Nay, ye fool, I've saved us.
He would have left home eventually, to get food or visit his uncle.
Even if he was imprisoned, he'd eventually escape and then disaster would surely follow.
But I know tha lad. He's so Lawful, if I command him ta stay away until I send fer him, he will—
Even if it means spendin' tha rest o' his life exiled!
Well, I hope ye know what yer doin'. 'Tis a risky business to screw wit prophecy.
Aye, don't I know it.
May Thor watch o'er him.
Aye, may the gods have mercy on his poor damned soul.
Beer?
Don't mind if I do.

Elan

Human bard
3 weeks ago

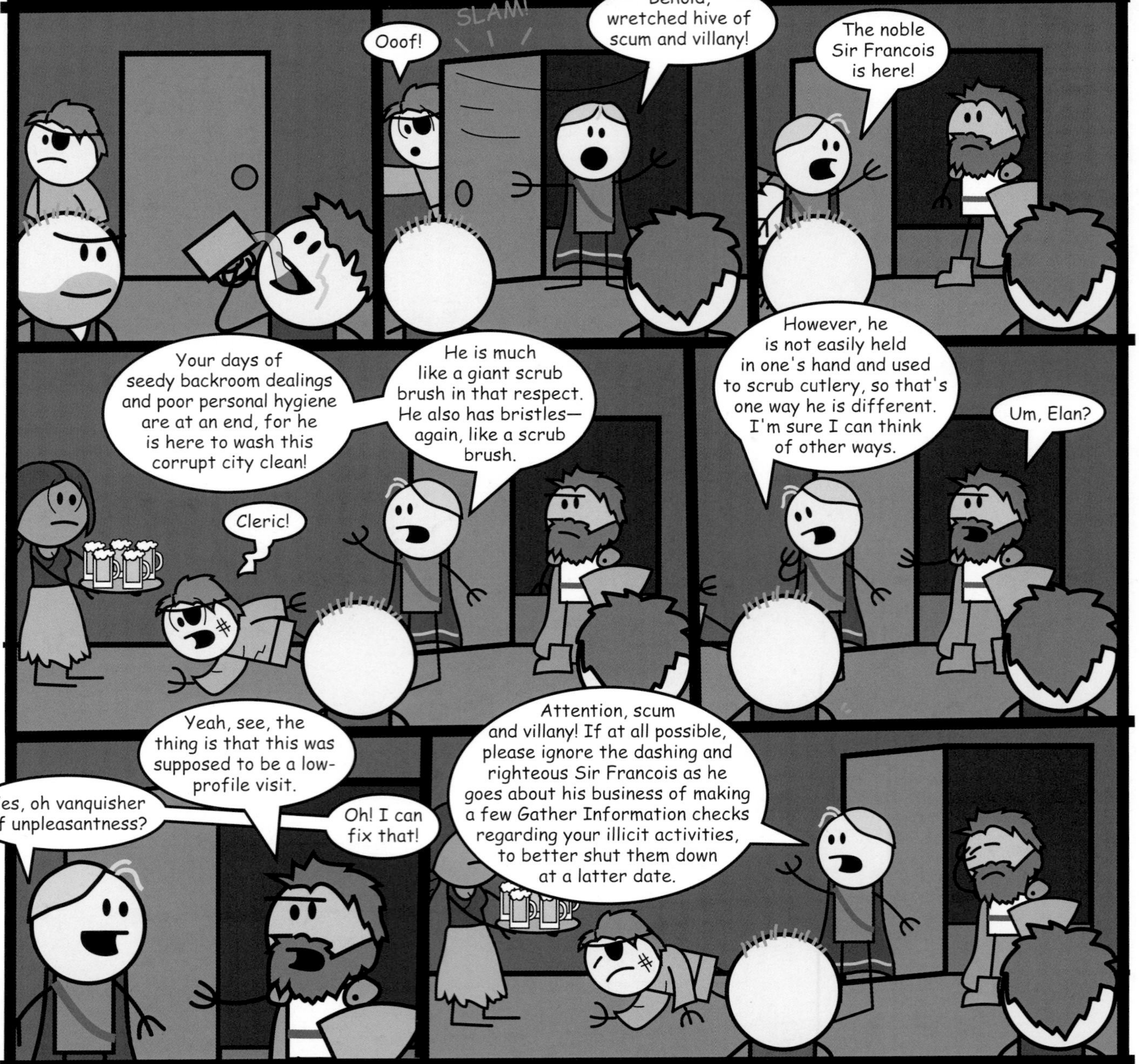

Ooof!
SLAM!
Behold, wretched hive of scum and villany!
The noble Sir Francois is here!
Your days of seedy backroom dealings and poor personal hygiene are at an end, for he is here to wash this corrupt city clean!
Cleric!
He is much like a giant scrub brush in that respect. He also has bristles—again, like a scrub brush.
However, he is not easily held in one's hand and used to scrub cutlery, so that's one way he is different. I'm sure I can think of other ways.
Um, Elan?
Yes, oh vanquisher of unpleasantness?
Yeah, see, the thing is that this was supposed to be a low-profile visit.
Oh! I can fix that!
Attention, scum and villany! If at all possible, please ignore the dashing and righteous Sir Francois as he goes about his business of making a few Gather Information checks regarding your illicit activities, to better shut them down at a latter date.

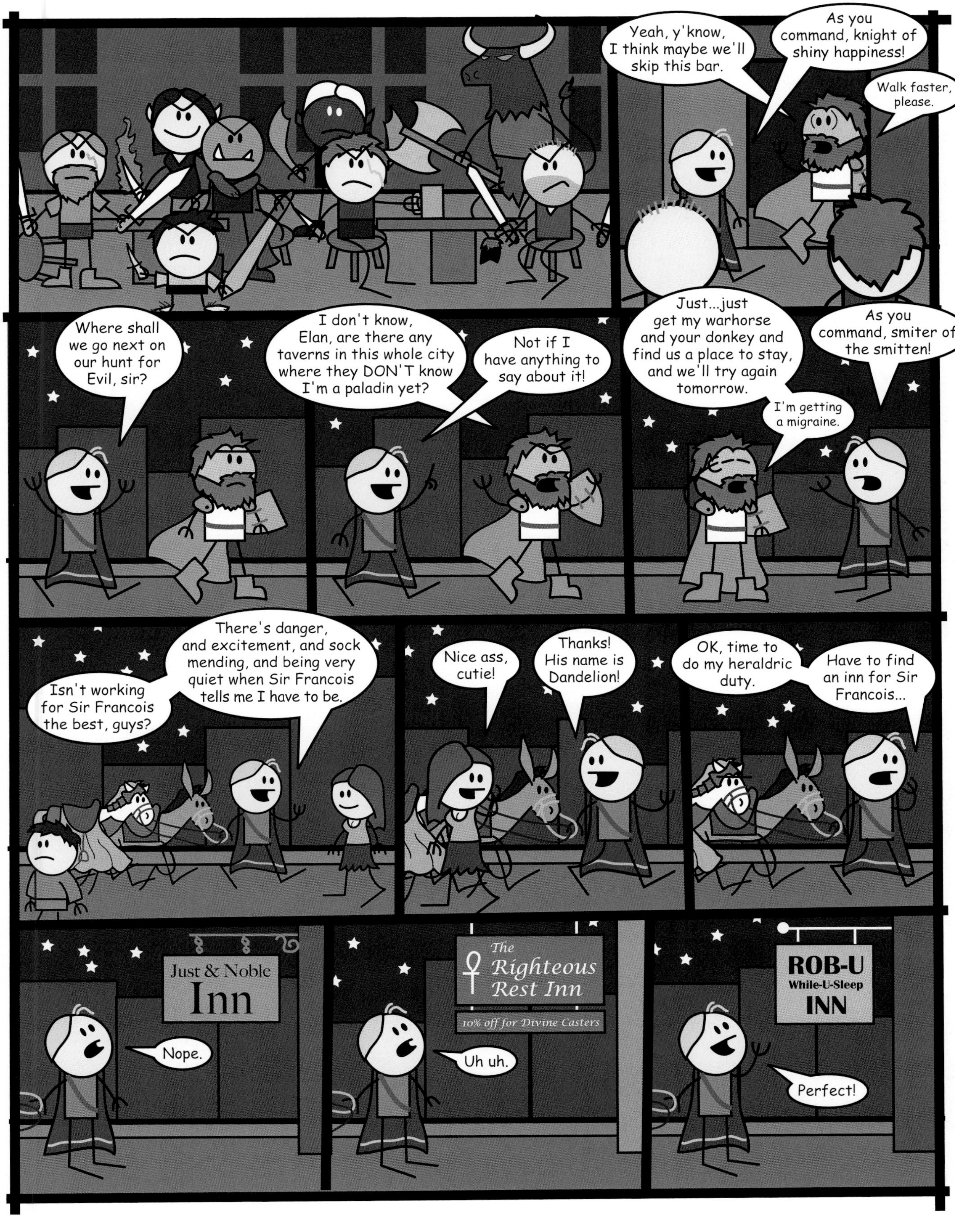
Yeah, y'know, I think maybe we'll skip this bar.
As you command, knight of shiny happiness!
Walk faster, please.
Where shall we go next on our hunt for Evil, sir?
I don't know, Elan, are there any taverns in this whole city where they DON'T know I'm a paladin yet?
Not if I have anything to say about it!
Just...just get my warhorse and your donkey and find us a place to stay, and we'll try again tomorrow.
I'm getting a migraine.
As you command, smiter of the smitten!
Isn't working for Sir Francois the best, guys?
There's danger, and excitement, and sock mending, and being very quiet when Sir Francois tells me I have to be.
Nice ass, cutie!
Thanks! His name is Dandelion!
OK, time to do my heraldric duty.
Have to find an inn for Sir Francois...
Just & Noble Inn
Nope.
The Righteous Rest Inn
10% off for Divine Casters
Uh uh.
ROB-U While-U-Sleep INN
Perfect!

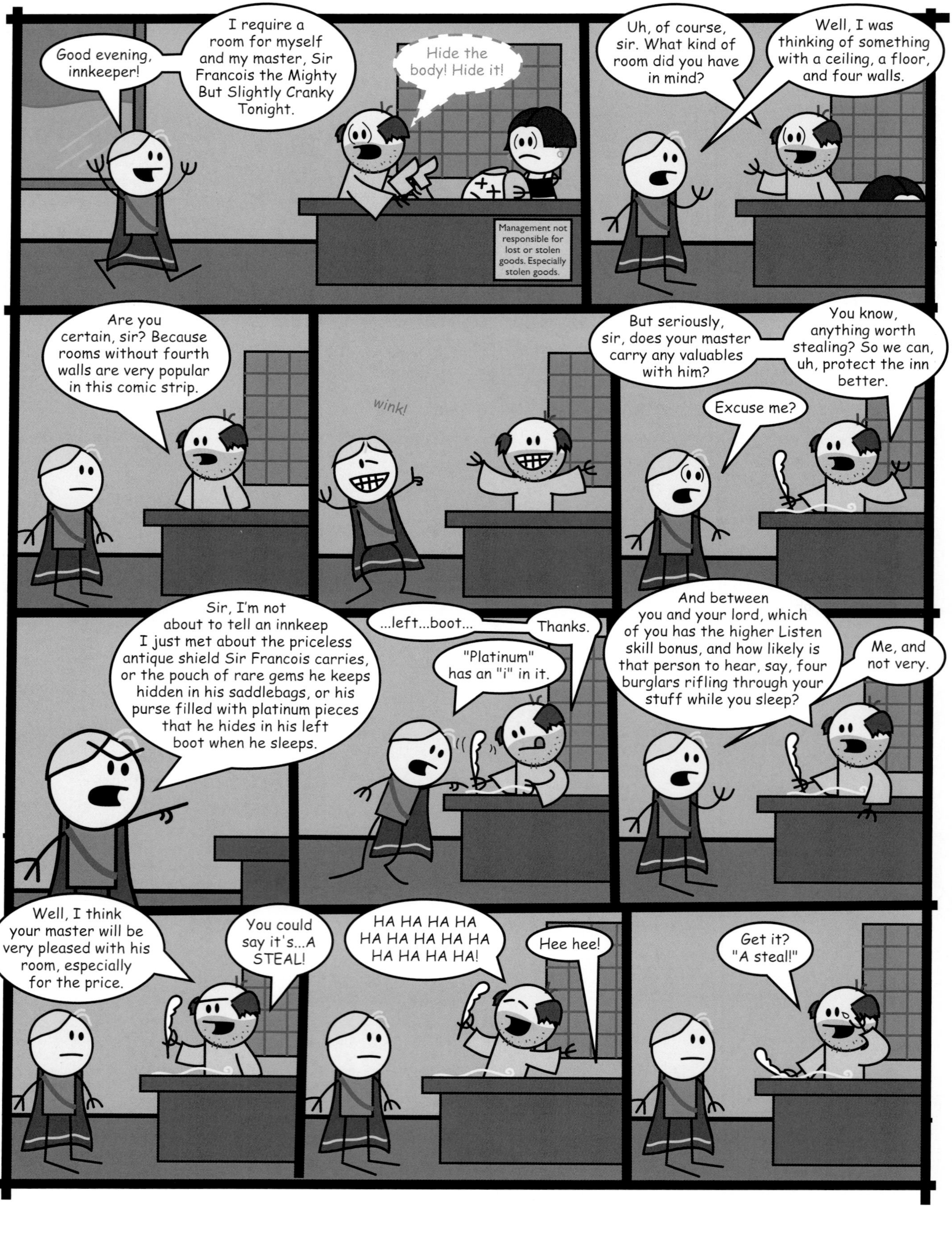
Good evening, innkeeper!
I require a room for myself and my master, Sir Francois the Mighty But Slightly Cranky Tonight.
Hide the body! Hide it!
Management not responsible for lost or stolen goods. Especially stolen goods.
Uh, of course, sir. What kind of room did you have in mind?
Well, I was thinking of something with a ceiling, a floor, and four walls.
Are you certain, sir? Because rooms without fourth walls are very popular in this comic strip.
wink!
But seriously, sir, does your master carry any valuables with him?
You know, anything worth stealing? So we can, uh, protect the inn better.
Excuse me?
Sir, I'm not about to tell an innkeep I just met about the priceless antique shield Sir Francois carries, or the pouch of rare gems he keeps hidden in his saddlebags, or his purse filled with platinum pieces that he hides in his left boot when he sleeps.
...left...boot...
Thanks.
"Platinum" has an "i" in it.
And between you and your lord, which of you has the higher Listen skill bonus, and how likely is that person to hear, say, four burglars rifling through your stuff while you sleep?
Me, and not very.
Well, I think your master will be very pleased with his room, especially for the price.
You could say it's...A STEAL!
HA HA HA HA HA HA HA HA HA HA HA HA HA!
Hee hee!
Get it? "A steal!"

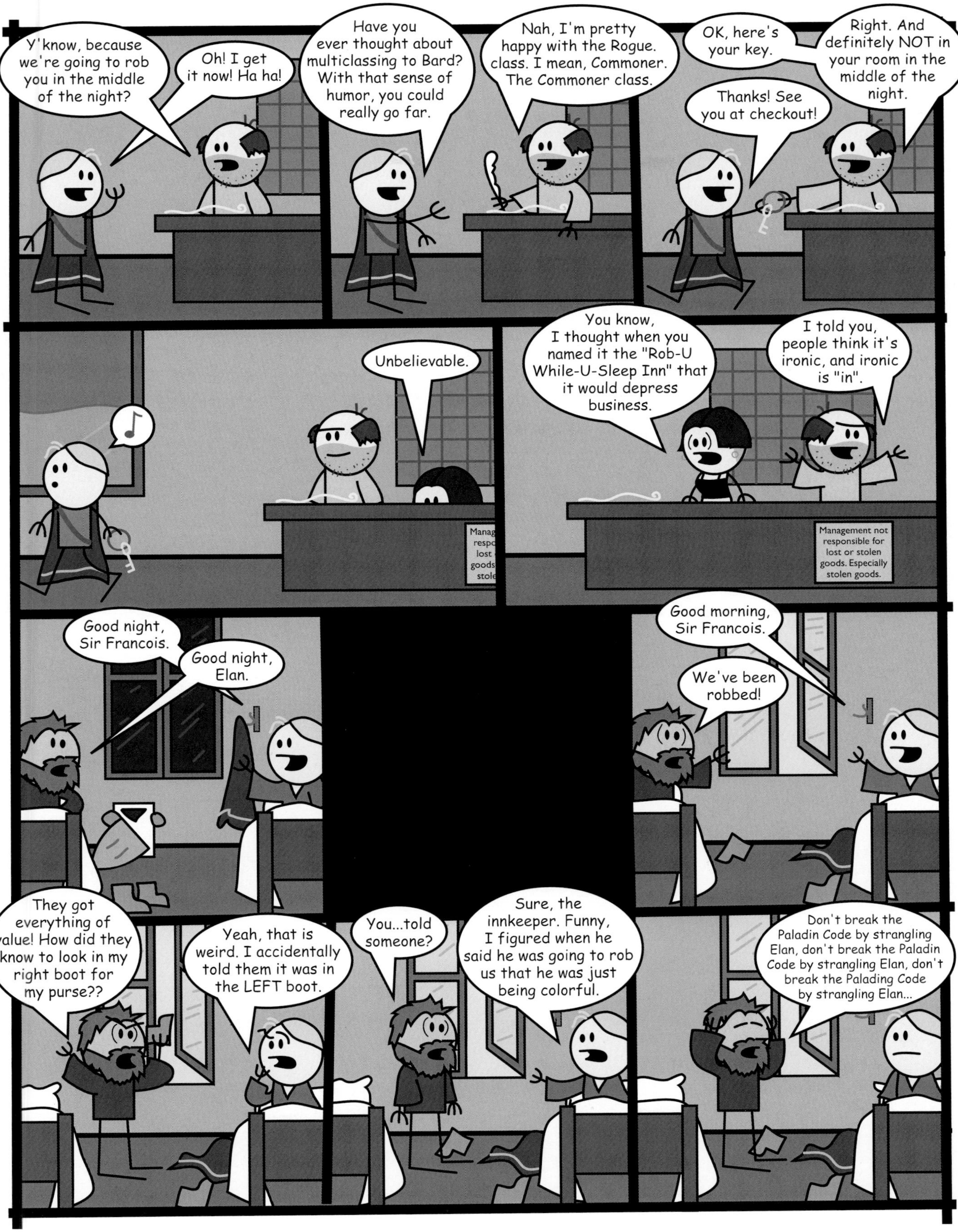
Y'know, because we're going to rob you in the middle of the night?
Oh! I get it now! Ha ha!
Have you ever thought about multiclassing to Bard? With that sense of humor, you could really go far.
Nah, I'm pretty happy with the Rogue. class. I mean, Commoner. The Commoner class.
OK, here's your key.
Right. And definitely NOT in your room in the middle of the night.
Thanks! See you at checkout!
Unbelievable.
You know, I thought when you named it the "Rob-U While-U-Sleep Inn" that it would depress business.
I told you, people think it's ironic, and ironic is "in".
Management not responsible for lost or stolen goods. Especially stolen goods.
Good night, Sir Francois.
Good night, Elan.
Good morning, Sir Francois.
We've been robbed!
They got everything of value! How did they know to look in my right boot for my purse??
Yeah, that is weird. I accidentally told them it was in the LEFT boot.
You...told someone?
Sure, the innkeeper. Funny, I figured when he said he was going to rob us that he was just being colorful.
Don't break the Paladin Code by strangling Elan, don't break the Paladin Code by strangling Elan, don't break the Palading Code by strangling Elan...

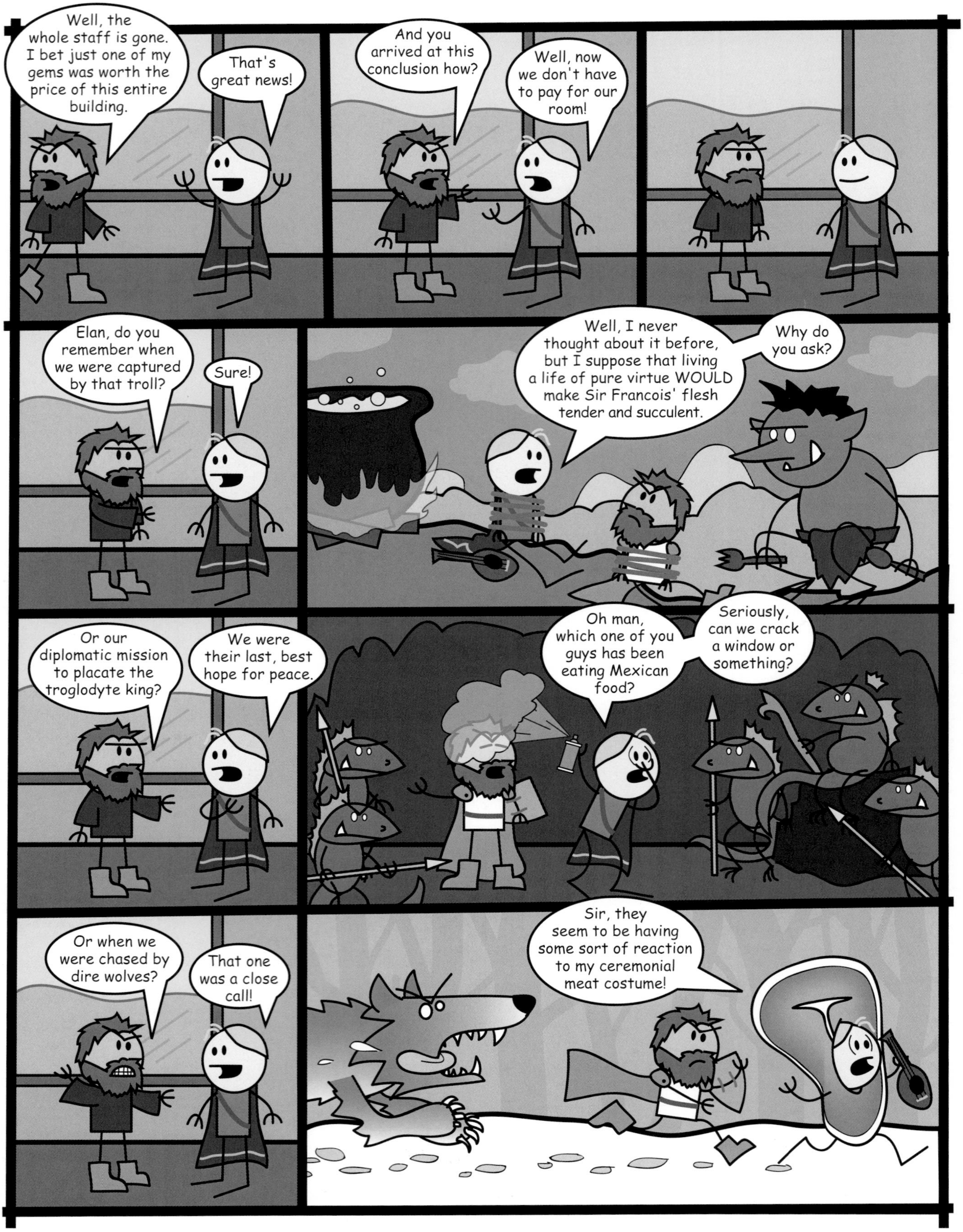
Well, the whole staff is gone. I bet just one of my gems was worth the price of this entire building.
That's great news!
And you arrived at this conclusion how?
Well, now we don't have to pay for our room!
Elan, do you remember when we were captured by that troll?
Sure!
Well, I never thought about it before, but I suppose that living a life of pure virtue WOULD make Sir Francois' flesh tender and succulent.
Why do you ask?
Or our diplomatic mission to placate the troglodyte king?
We were their last, best hope for peace.
Oh man, which one of you guys has been eating Mexican food?
Seriously, can we crack a window or something?
Or when we were chased by dire wolves?
That one was a close call!
Sir, they seem to be having some sort of reaction to my ceremonial meat costume!

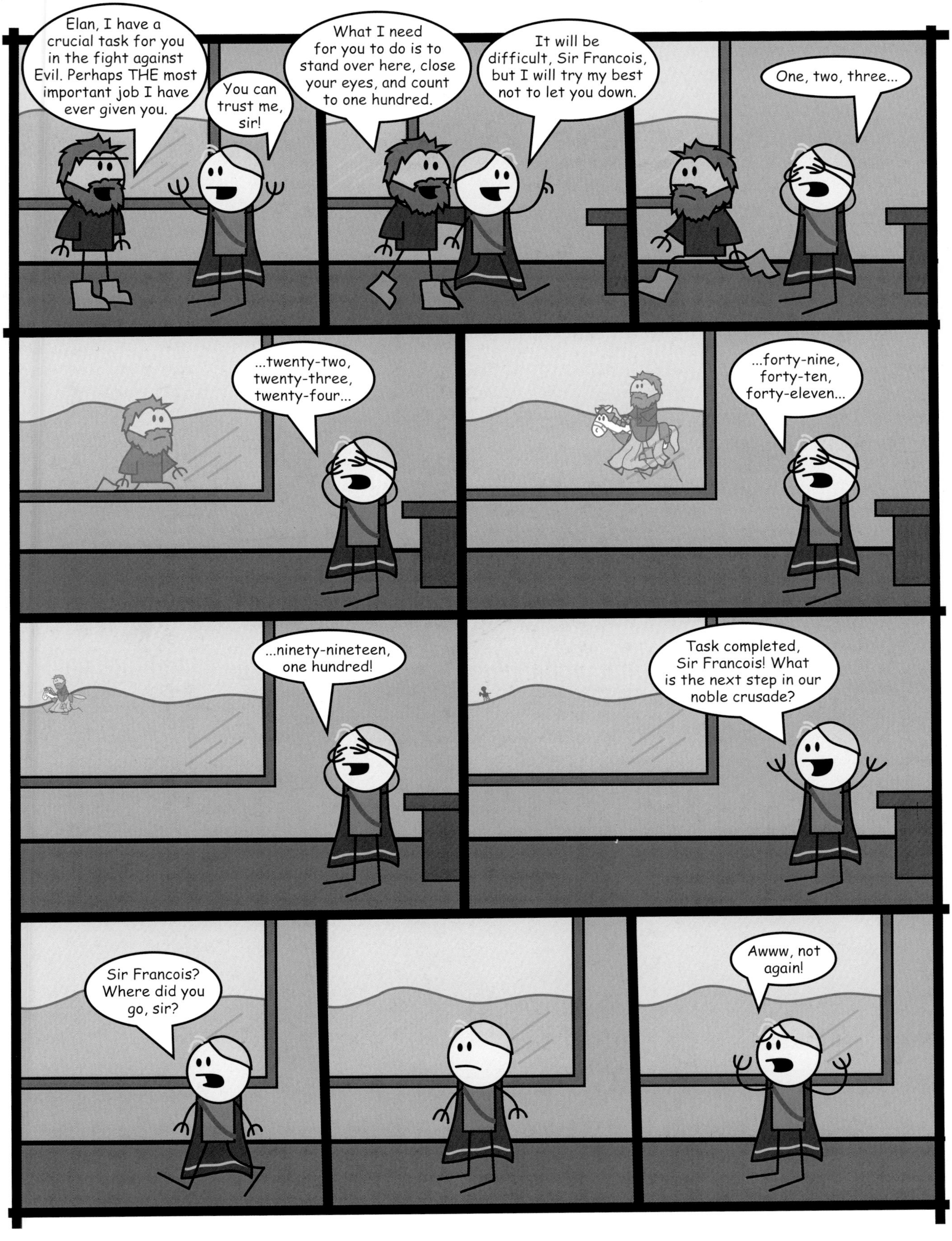
Elan, I have a crucial task for you in the fight against Evil. Perhaps THE most important job I have ever given you.
You can trust me, sir!
What I need for you to do is to stand over here, close your eyes, and count to one hundred.
It will be difficult, Sir Francois, but I will try my best not to let you down.
One, two, three...
...twenty-two, twenty-three, twenty-four...
...forty-nine, forty-ten, forty-eleven...
...ninety-nineteen, one hundred!
Task completed, Sir Francois! What is the next step in our noble crusade?
Sir Francois? Where did you go, sir?
Awww, not again!

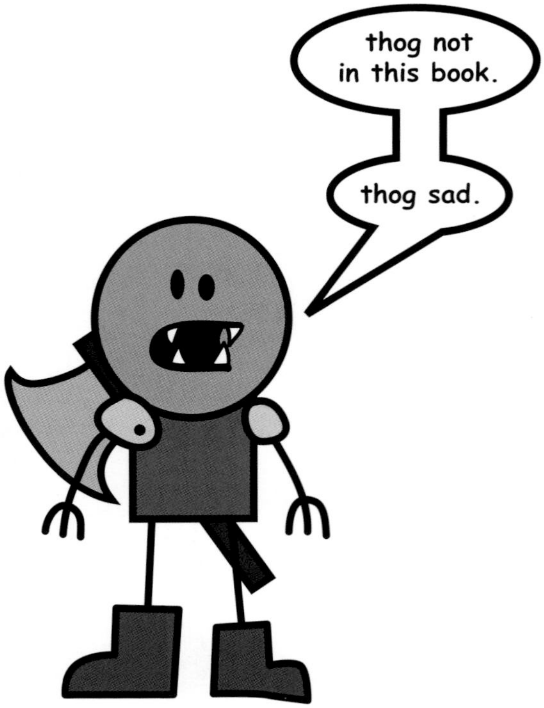
thog not
in this book.
thog sad.

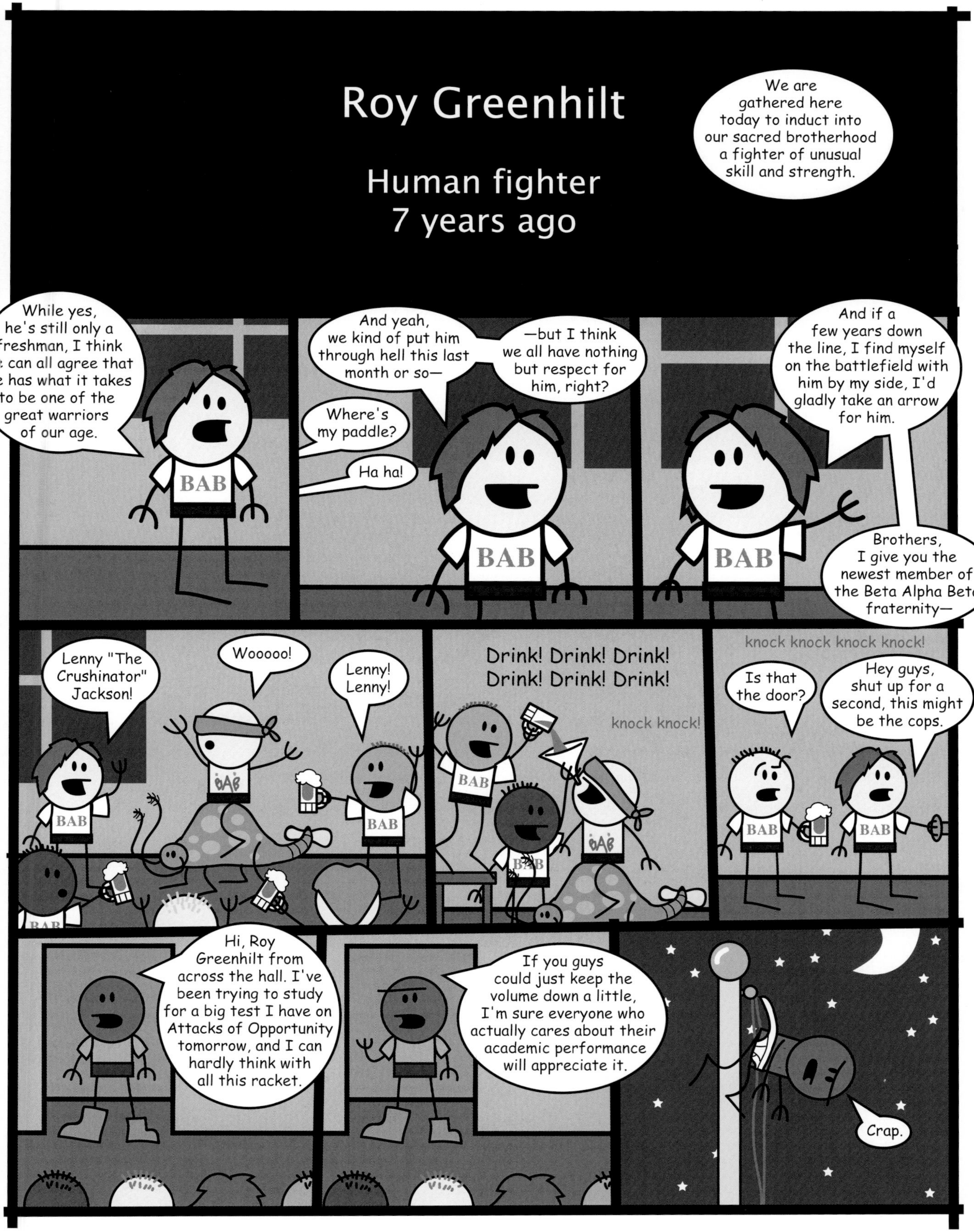
Roy Greenhilt
Human fighter
7 years ago
We are gathered here today to induct into our sacred brotherhood a fighter of unusual skill and strength.
While yes, he's still only a freshman, I think we can all agree that he has what it takes to be one of the great warriors of our age.
And yeah, we kind of put him through hell this last month or so—
Where's my paddle?
Ha ha!
—but I think we all have nothing but respect for him, right?
And if a few years down the line, I find myself on the battlefield with him by my side, I'd gladly take an arrow for him.
Brothers, I give you the newest member of the Beta Alpha Beta fraternity—
Lenny "The Crushinator" Jackson!
Wooooo!
Lenny! Lenny!
Drink! Drink! Drink! Drink! Drink! Drink!
knock knock!
knock knock knock knock!
Is that the door?
Hey guys, shut up for a second, this might be the cops.
Hi, Roy Greenhilt from across the hall. I've been trying to study for a big test I have on Attacks of Opportunity tomorrow, and I can hardly think with all this racket.
If you guys could just keep the volume down a little, I'm sure everyone who actually cares about their academic performance will appreciate it.
Crap.

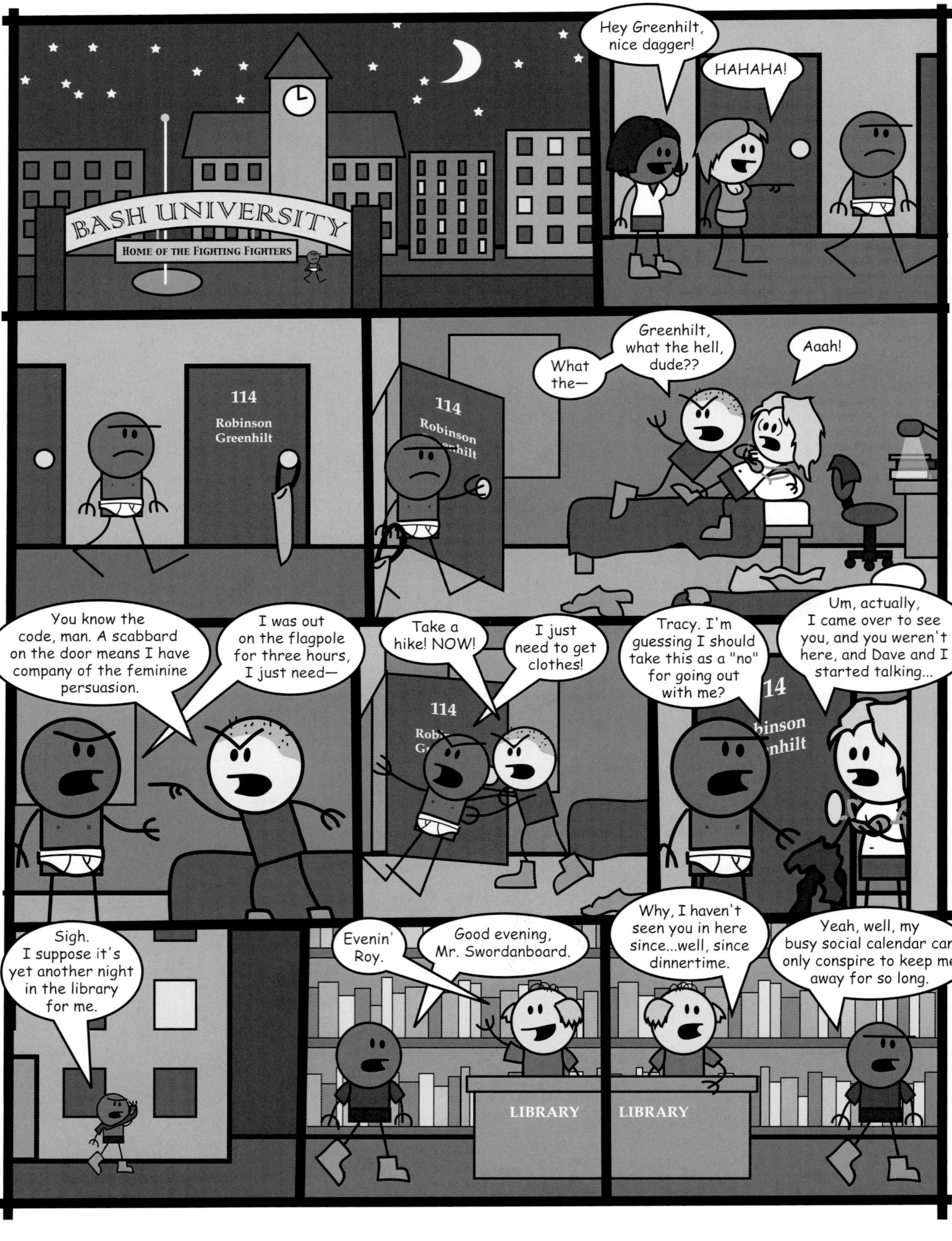
BASH UNIVERSITY
HOME OF THE FIGHTING FIGHTERS
Hey Greenhilt, nice dagger!
HAHAHA!
114
Robinson
Greenhilt
114
Robinson
Greenhilt
What the—
Greenhilt, what the hell, dude??
Aaah!
You know the code, man. A scabbard on the door means I have company of the feminine persuasion.
I was out on the flagpole for three hours, I just need—
Take a hike! NOW!
I just need to get clothes!
Tracy. I'm guessing I should take this as a "no" for going out with me?
Um, actually, I came over to see you, and you weren't here, and Dave and I started talking...
Sigh. I suppose it's yet another night in the library for me.
Evenin' Roy.
Good evening, Mr. Swordanboard.
LIBRARY
Why, I haven't seen you in here since...well, since dinnertime.
LIBRARY
Yeah, well, my busy social calendar can only conspire to keep me away for so long.

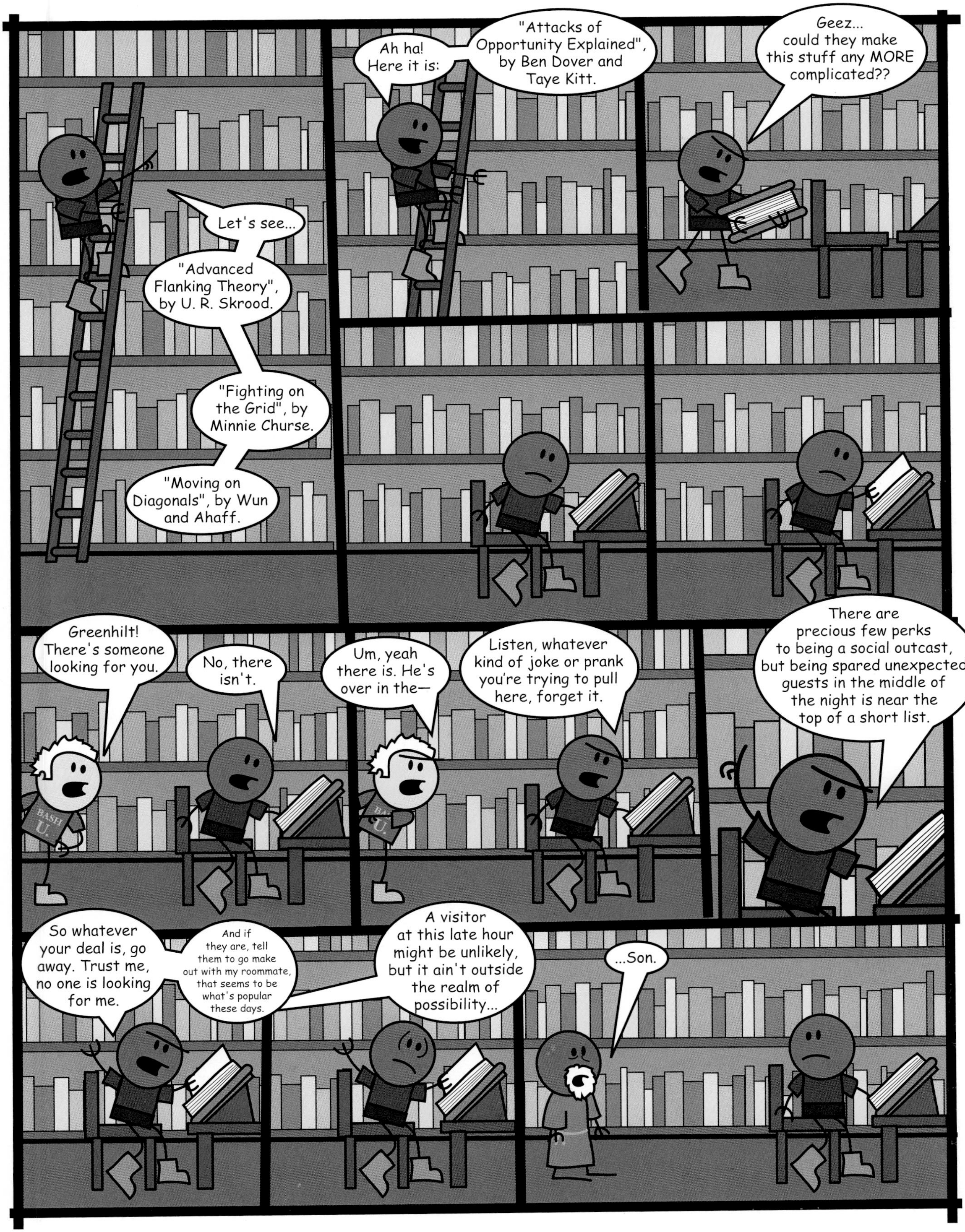
Let's see...
"Advanced Flanking Theory", by U. R. Skrood.
"Fighting on the Grid", by Minnie Churse.
"Moving on Diagonals", by Wun and Ahaff.
Ah ha! Here it is:
"Attacks of Opportunity Explained", by Ben Dover and Taye Kitt.
Geez... could they make this stuff any MORE complicated??
Greenhilt! There's someone looking for you.
BASH U.
No, there isn't.
Um, yeah there is. He's over in the—
Listen, whatever kind of joke or prank you're trying to pull here, forget it.
There are precious few perks to being a social outcast, but being spared unexpected guests in the middle of the night is near the top of a short list.
So whatever your deal is, go away. Trust me, no one is looking for me.
And if they are, tell them to go make out with my roommate, that seems to be what's popular these days.
A visitor at this late hour might be unlikely, but it ain't outside the realm of possibility...
...Son.

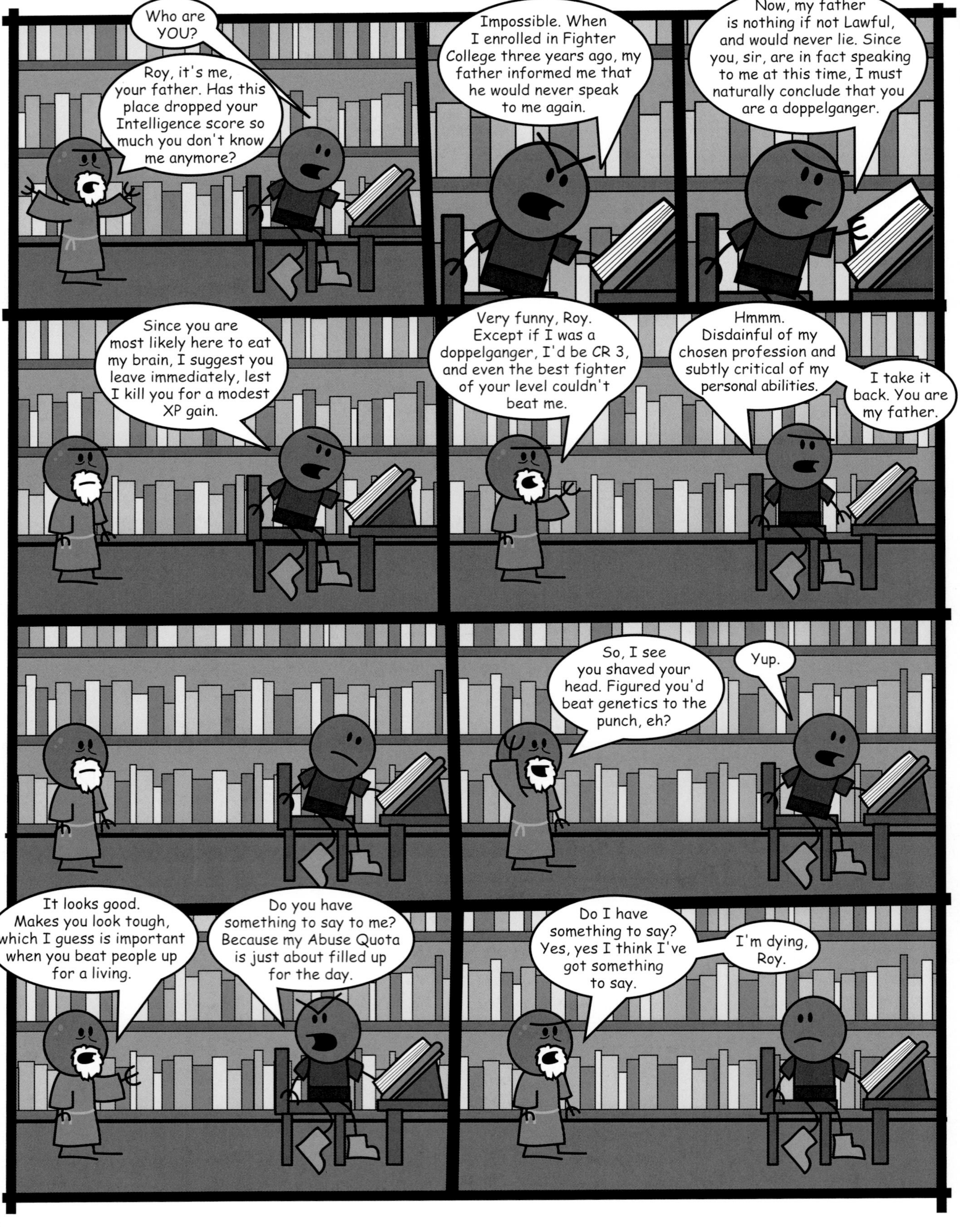
Who are YOU?
Roy, it's me, your father. Has this place dropped your Intelligence score so much you don't know me anymore?
Impossible. When I enrolled in Fighter College three years ago, my father informed me that he would never speak to me again.
Now, my father is nothing if not Lawful, and would never lie. Since you, sir, are in fact speaking to me at this time, I must naturally conclude that you are a doppelganger.
Since you are most likely here to eat my brain, I suggest you leave immediately, lest I kill you for a modest XP gain.
Very funny, Roy. Except if I was a doppelganger, I'd be CR 3, and even the best fighter of your level couldn't beat me.
Hmmm. Disdainful of my chosen profession and subtly critical of my personal abilities.
I take it back. You are my father.
So, I see you shaved your head. Figured you'd beat genetics to the punch, eh?
Yup.
It looks good. Makes you look tough, which I guess is important when you beat people up for a living.
Do you have something to say to me? Because my Abuse Quota is just about filled up for the day.
Do I have something to say? Yes, yes I think I've got something to say.
I'm dying, Roy.

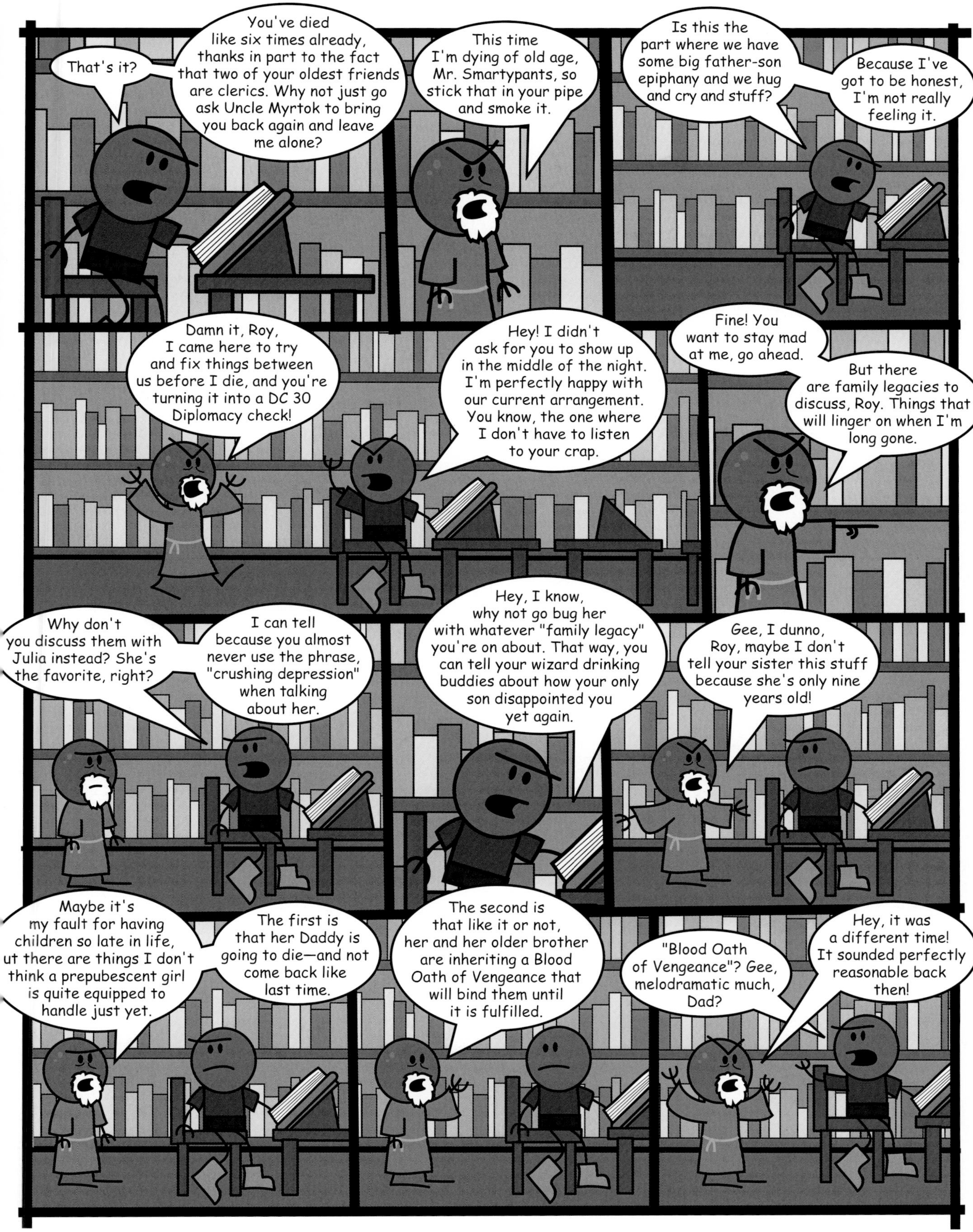
That's it?
You've died like six times already, thanks in part to the fact that two of your oldest friends are clerics. Why not just go ask Uncle Myrtok to bring you back again and leave me alone?
This time I'm dying of old age, Mr. Smartypants, so stick that in your pipe and smoke it.
Is this the part where we have some big father-son epiphany and we hug and cry and stuff?
Because I've got to be honest, I'm not really feeling it.
Damn it, Roy, I came here to try and fix things between us before I die, and you're turning it into a DC 30 Diplomacy check!
Hey! I didn't ask for you to show up in the middle of the night. I'm perfectly happy with our current arrangement. You know, the one where I don't have to listen to your crap.
Fine! You want to stay mad at me, go ahead.
But there are family legacies to discuss, Roy. Things that will linger on when I'm long gone.
Why don't you discuss them with Julia instead? She's the favorite, right?
I can tell because you almost never use the phrase, "crushing depression" when talking about her.
Hey, I know, why not go bug her with whatever "family legacy" you're on about. That way, you can tell your wizard drinking buddies about how your only son disappointed you yet again.
Gee, I dunno, Roy, maybe I don't tell your sister this stuff because she's only nine years old!
Maybe it's my fault for having children so late in life, ut there are things I don't think a prepubescent girl is quite equipped to handle just yet.
The first is that her Daddy is going to die—and not come back like last time.
The second is that like it or not, her and her older brother are inheriting a Blood Oath of Vengeance that will bind them until it is fulfilled.
"Blood Oath of Vengeance"? Gee, melodramatic much, Dad?
Hey, it was a different time! It sounded perfectly reasonable back then!

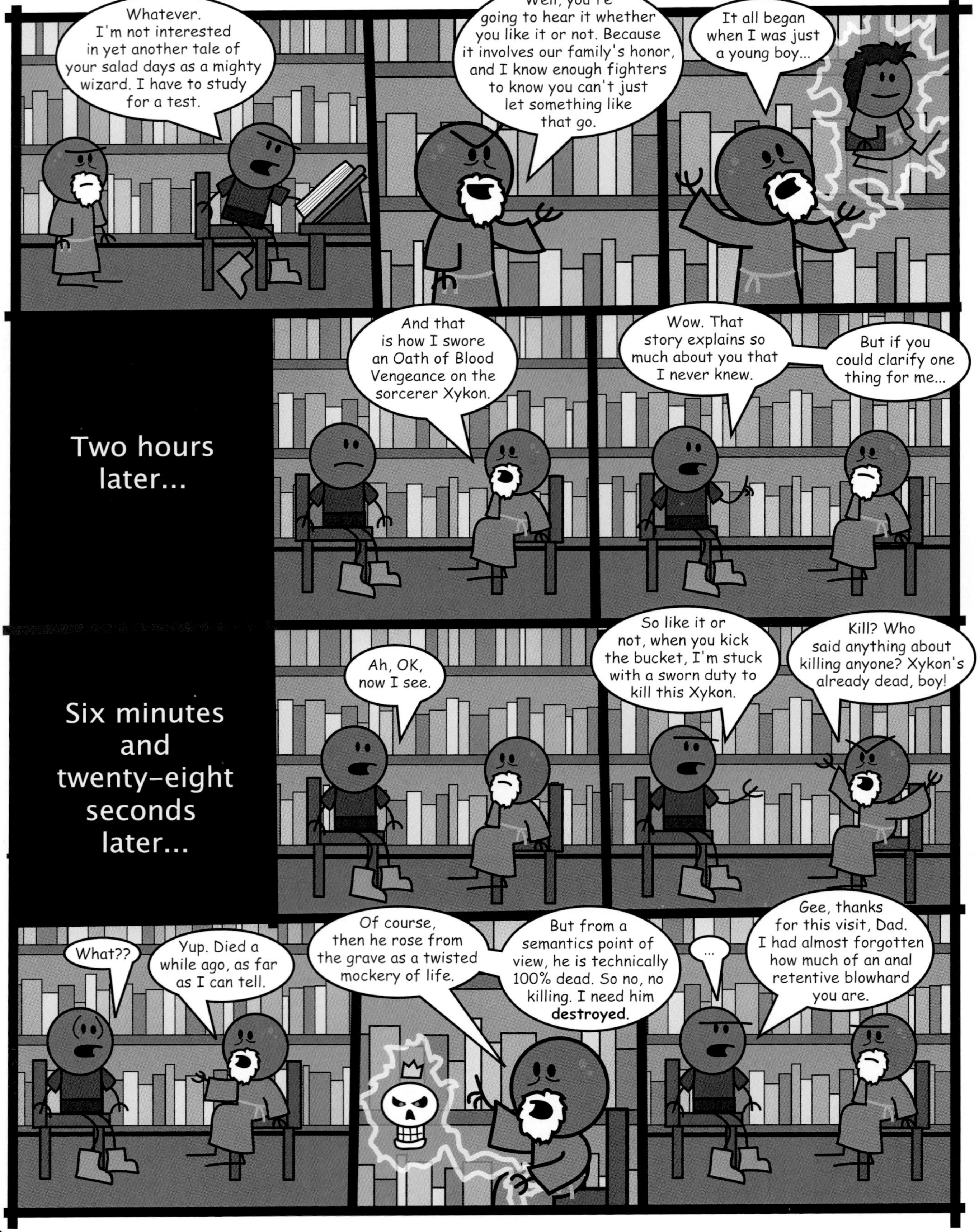
Whatever. I'm not interested in yet another tale of your salad days as a mighty wizard. I have to study for a test.
Well, you're going to hear it whether you like it or not. Because it involves our family's honor, and I know enough fighters to know you can't just let something like that go.
It all began when I was just a young boy...
Two hours later...
And that is how I swore an Oath of Blood Vengeance on the sorcerer Xykon.
Wow. That story explains so much about you that I never knew.
But if you could clarify one thing for me...
Six minutes and twenty-eight seconds later...
Ah, OK, now I see.
So like it or not, when you kick the bucket, I'm stuck with a sworn duty to kill this Xykon.
Kill? Who said anything about killing anyone? Xykon's already dead, boy!
What??
Yup. Died a while ago, as far as I can tell.
Of course, then he rose from the grave as a twisted mockery of life.
But from a semantics point of view, he is technically 100% dead. So no, no killing. I need him **destroyed**.
...
Gee, thanks for this visit, Dad. I had almost forgotten how much of an anal retentive blowhard you are.

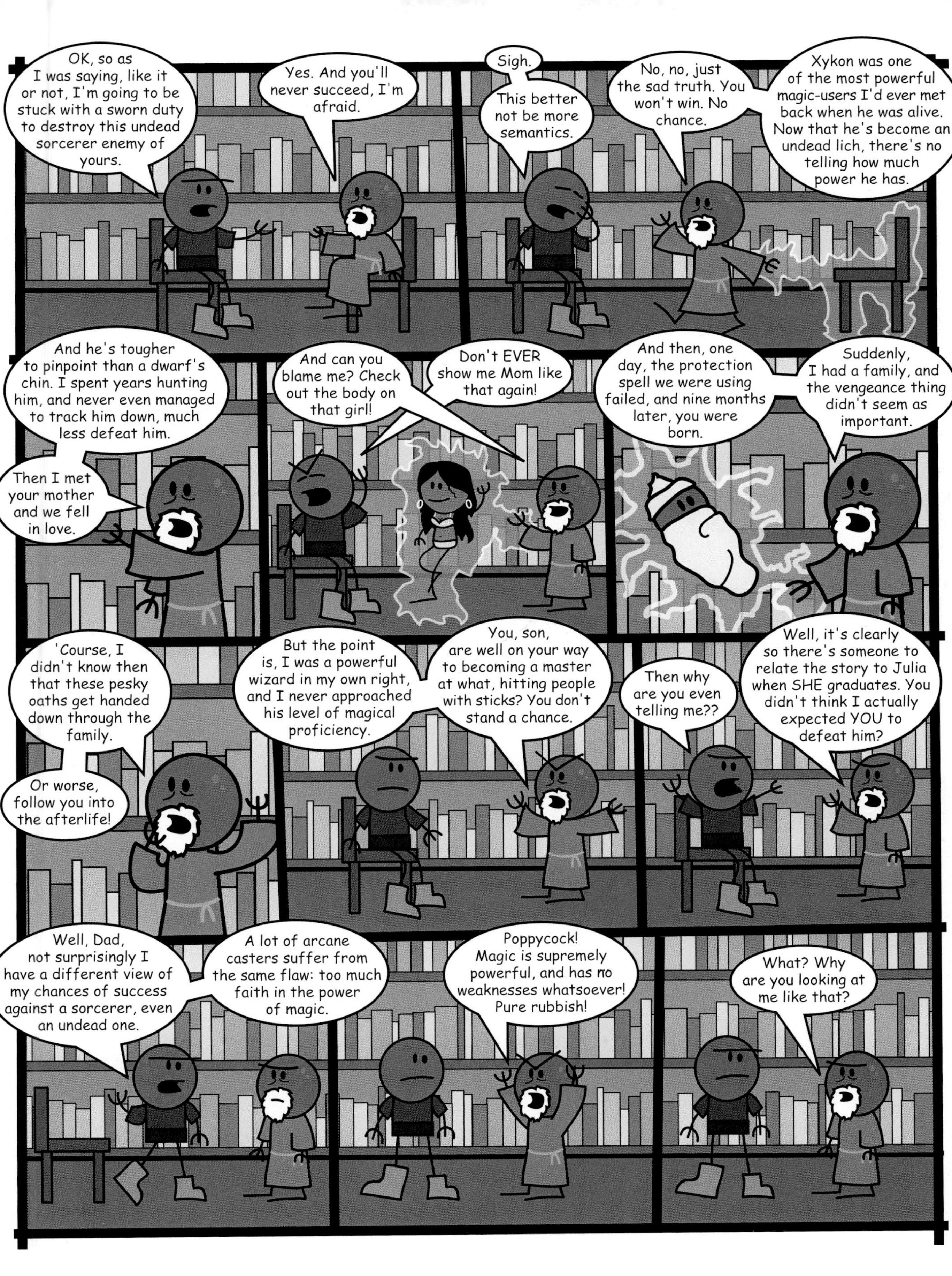
OK, so as I was saying, like it or not, I'm going to be stuck with a sworn duty to destroy this undead sorcerer enemy of yours.
Yes. And you'll never succeed, I'm afraid.
Sigh.
This better not be more semantics.
No, no, just the sad truth. You won't win. No chance.
Xykon was one of the most powerful magic-users I'd ever met back when he was alive. Now that he's become an undead lich, there's no telling how much power he has.
And he's tougher to pinpoint than a dwarf's chin. I spent years hunting him, and never even managed to track him down, much less defeat him.
Then I met your mother and we fell in love.
And can you blame me? Check out the body on that girl!
Don't EVER show me Mom like that again!
And then, one day, the protection spell we were using failed, and nine months later, you were born.
Suddenly, I had a family, and the vengeance thing didn't seem as important.
'Course, I didn't know then that these pesky oaths get handed down through the family.
Or worse, follow you into the afterlife!
But the point is, I was a powerful wizard in my own right, and I never approached his level of magical proficiency.
You, son, are well on your way to becoming a master at what, hitting people with sticks? You don't stand a chance.
Then why are you even telling me??
Well, it's clearly so there's someone to relate the story to Julia when SHE graduates. You didn't think I actually expected YOU to defeat him?
Well, Dad, not surprisingly I have a different view of my chances of success against a sorcerer, even an undead one.
A lot of arcane casters suffer from the same flaw: too much faith in the power of magic.
Poppycock! Magic is supremely powerful, and has no weaknesses whatsoever! Pure rubbish!
What? Why are you looking at me like that?

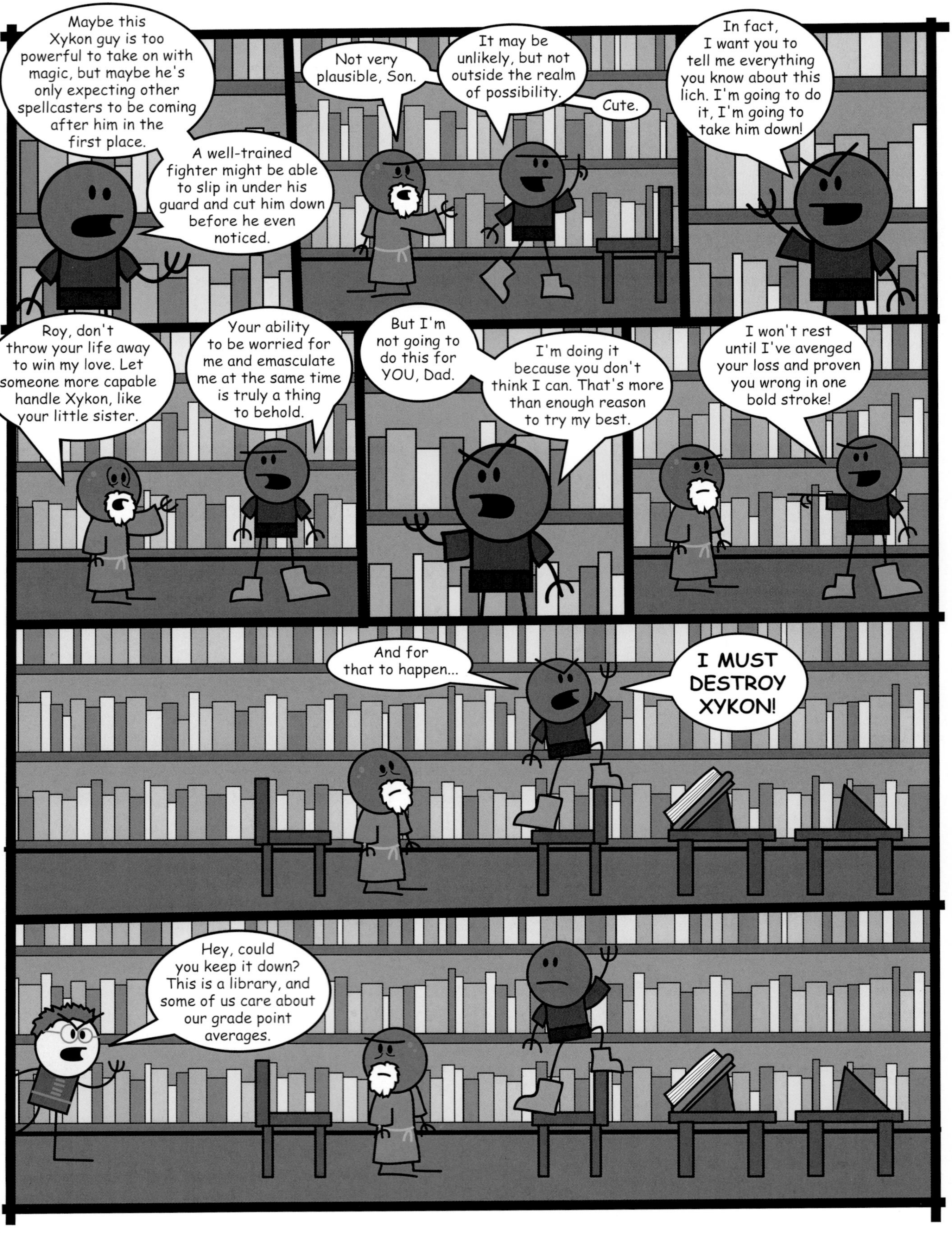
Maybe this Xykon guy is too powerful to take on with magic, but maybe he's only expecting other spellcasters to be coming after him in the first place.
A well-trained fighter might be able to slip in under his guard and cut him down before he even noticed.
Not very plausible, Son.
It may be unlikely, but not outside the realm of possibility.
Cute.
In fact, I want you to tell me everything you know about this lich. I'm going to do it, I'm going to take him down!
Roy, don't throw your life away to win my love. Let someone more capable handle Xykon, like your little sister.
Your ability to be worried for me and emasculate me at the same time is truly a thing to behold.
But I'm not going to do this for YOU, Dad.
I'm doing it because you don't think I can. That's more than enough reason to try my best.
I won't rest until I've avenged your loss and proven you wrong in one bold stroke!
And for that to happen...
I MUST DESTROY XYKON!
Hey, could you keep it down? This is a library, and some of us care about our grade point averages.

Belkar Bitterleaf

Halfling ranger
4 days ago

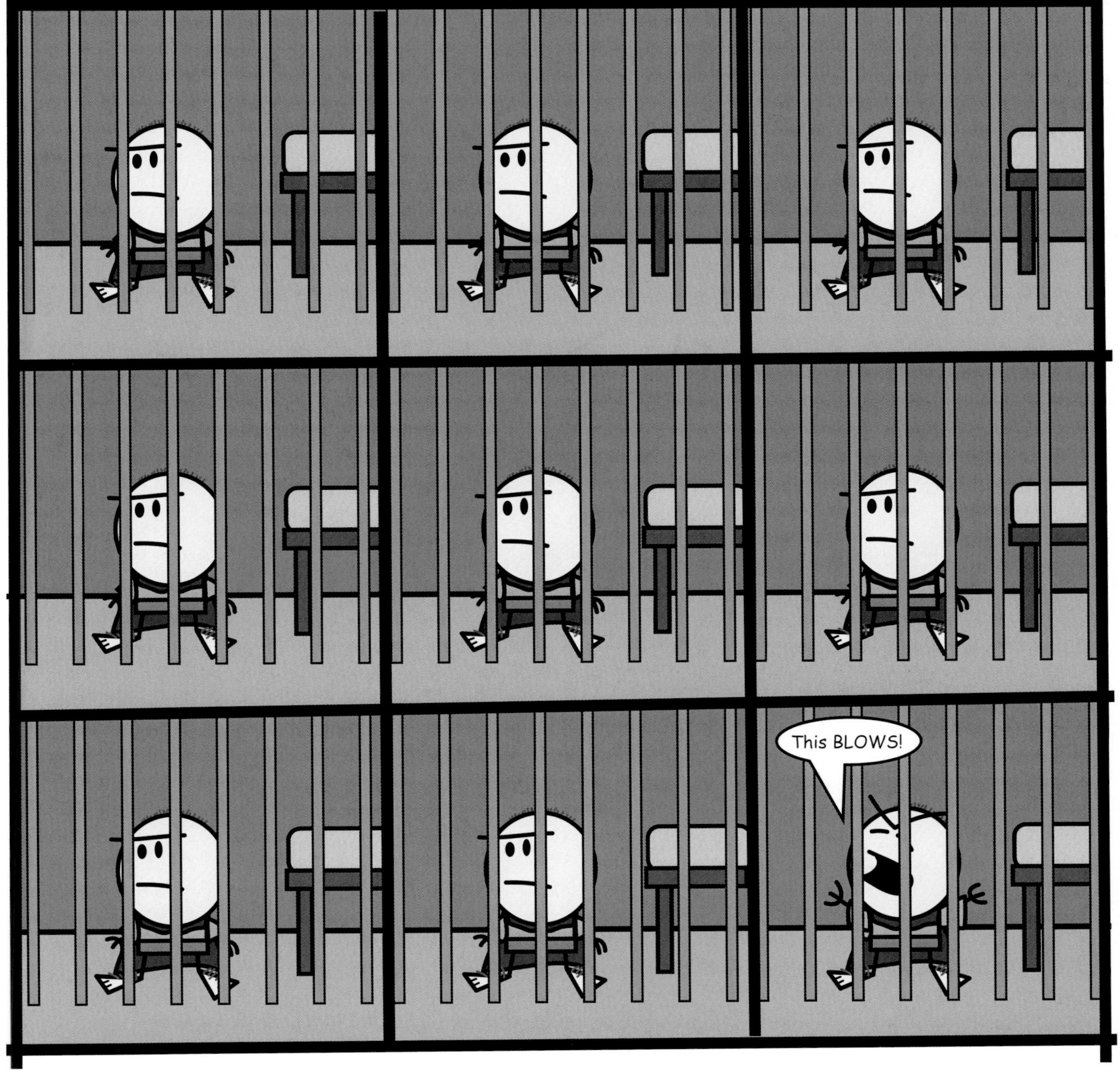
This BLOWS!

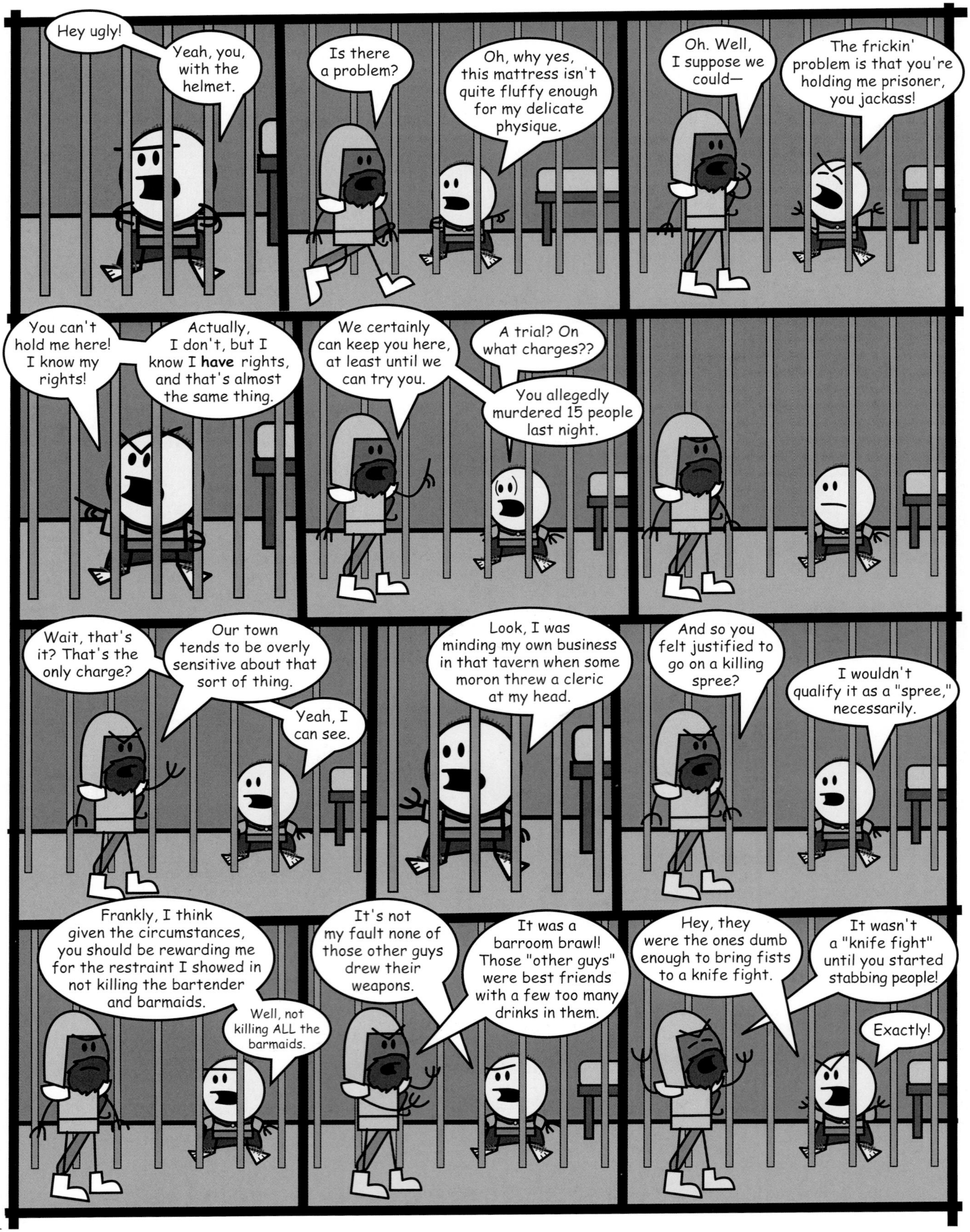

Hey ugly!
Yeah, you, with the helmet.
Is there a problem?
Oh, why yes, this mattress isn't quite fluffy enough for my delicate physique.
Oh. Well, I suppose we could—
The frickin' problem is that you're holding me prisoner, you jackass!
You can't hold me here! I know my rights!
Actually, I don't, but I know I **have** rights, and that's almost the same thing.
We certainly can keep you here, at least until we can try you.
A trial? On what charges??
You allegedly murdered 15 people last night.
Wait, that's it? That's the only charge?
Our town tends to be overly sensitive about that sort of thing.
Yeah, I can see.
Look, I was minding my own business in that tavern when some moron threw a cleric at my head.
And so you felt justified to go on a killing spree?
I wouldn't qualify it as a "spree," necessarily.
Frankly, I think given the circumstances, you should be rewarding me for the restraint I showed in not killing the bartender and barmaids.
Well, not killing ALL the barmaids.
It's not my fault none of those other guys drew their weapons.
It was a barroom brawl! Those "other guys" were best friends with a few too many drinks in them.
Hey, they were the ones dumb enough to bring fists to a knife fight.
It wasn't a "knife fight" until you started stabbing people!
Exactly!

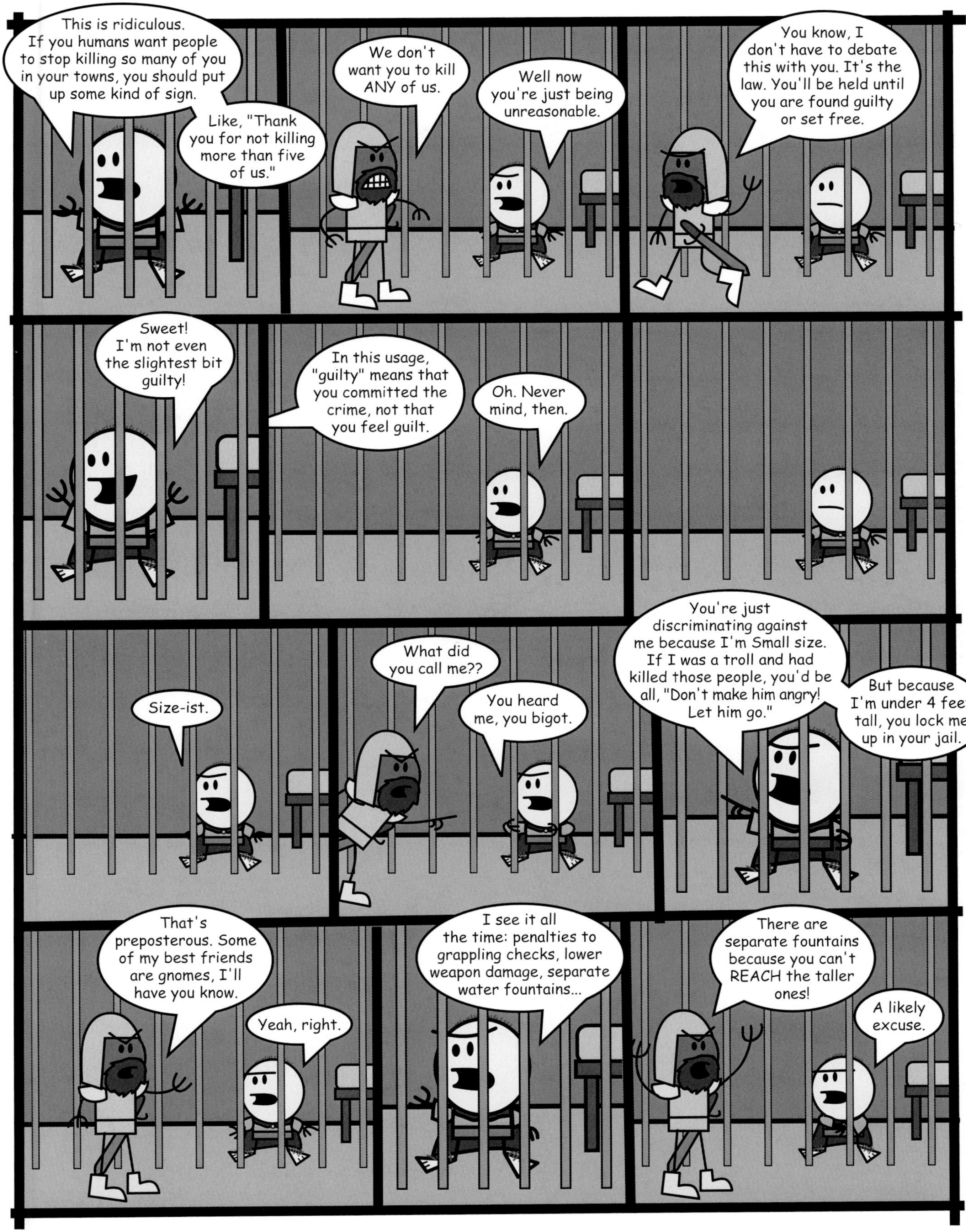
This is ridiculous. If you humans want people to stop killing so many of you in your towns, you should put up some kind of sign.
Like, "Thank you for not killing more than five of us."
We don't want you to kill ANY of us.
Well now you're just being unreasonable.
You know, I don't have to debate this with you. It's the law. You'll be held until you are found guilty or set free.
Sweet! I'm not even the slightest bit guilty!
In this usage, "guilty" means that you committed the crime, not that you feel guilt.
Oh. Never mind, then.
Size-ist.
What did you call me??
You heard me, you bigot.
You're just discriminating against me because I'm Small size. If I was a troll and had killed those people, you'd be all, "Don't make him angry! Let him go."
But because I'm under 4 feet tall, you lock me up in your jail.
That's preposterous. Some of my best friends are gnomes, I'll have you know.
Yeah, right.
I see it all the time: penalties to grappling checks, lower weapon damage, separate water fountains...
There are separate fountains because you can't REACH the taller ones!
A likely excuse.

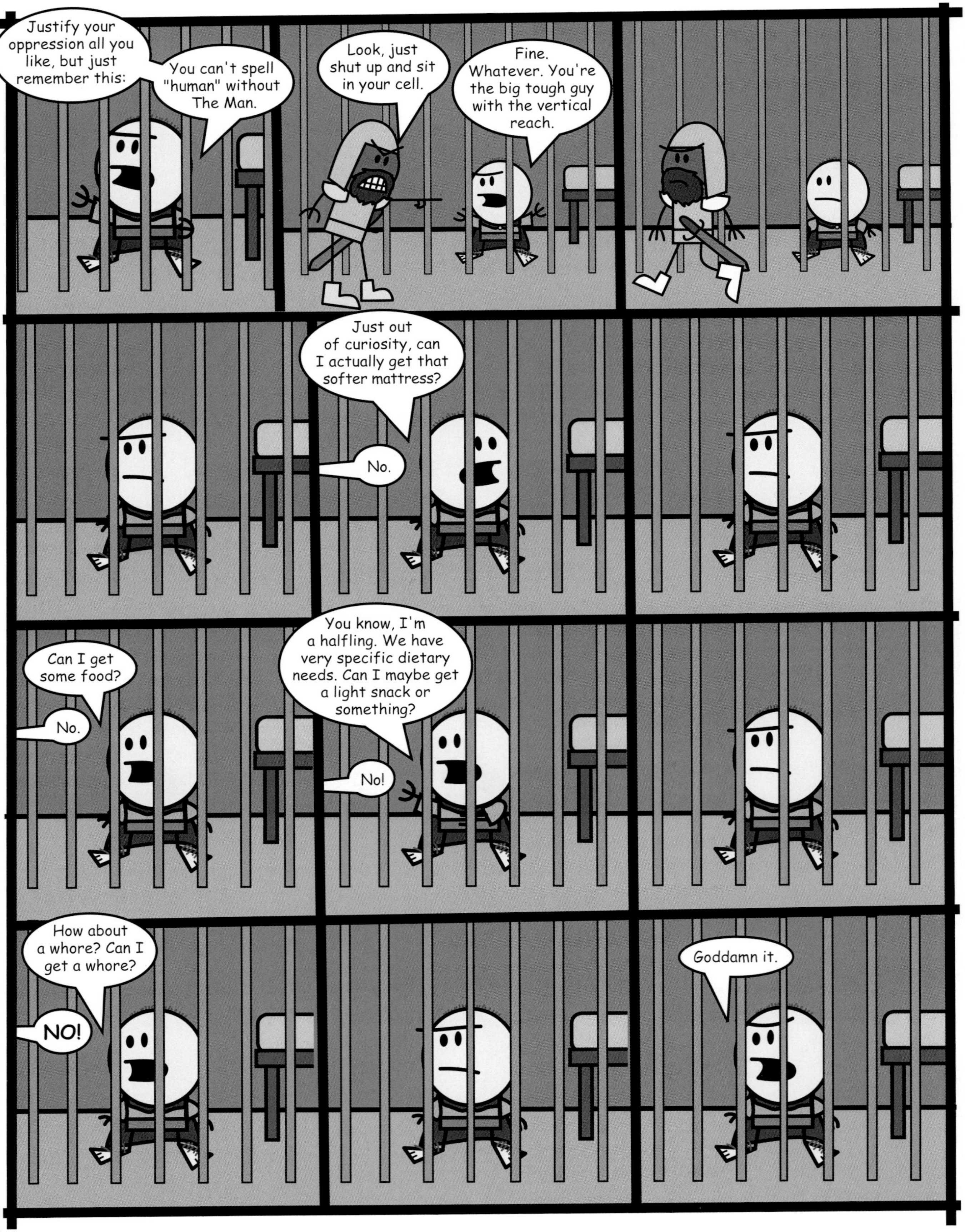
Justify your oppression all you like, but just remember this:
You can't spell "human" without The Man.
Look, just shut up and sit in your cell.
Fine. Whatever. You're the big tough guy with the vertical reach.
Just out of curiosity, can I actually get that softer mattress?
No.
Can I get some food?
No.
You know, I'm a halfling. We have very specific dietary needs. Can I maybe get a light snack or something?
No!
How about a whore? Can I get a whore?
NO!
Goddamn it.

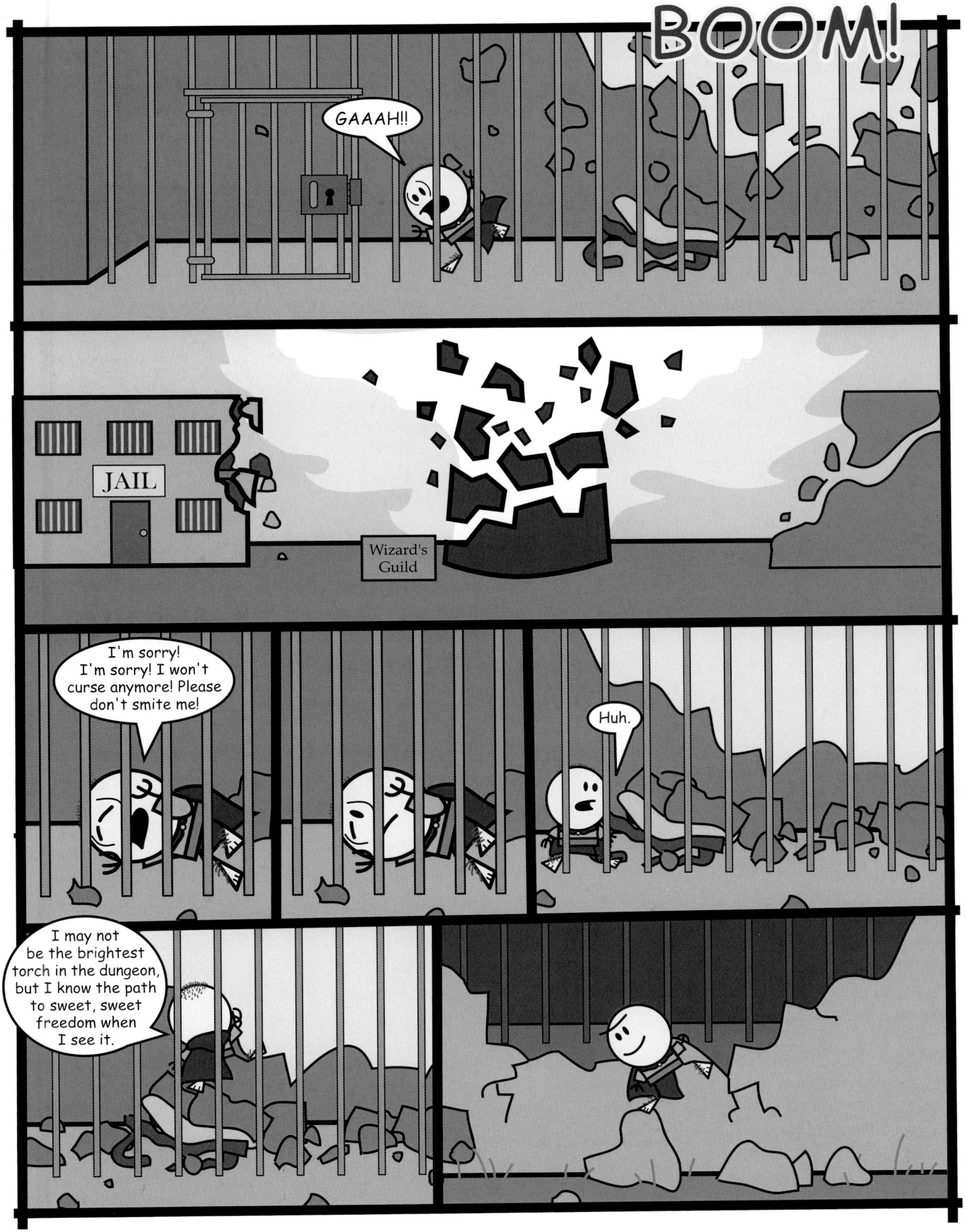
BOOM!
GAAAH!!
JAIL
Wizard's Guild
I'm sorry! I'm sorry! I won't curse anymore! Please don't smite me!
Huh.
I may not be the brightest torch in the dungeon, but I know the path to sweet, sweet freedom when I see it.

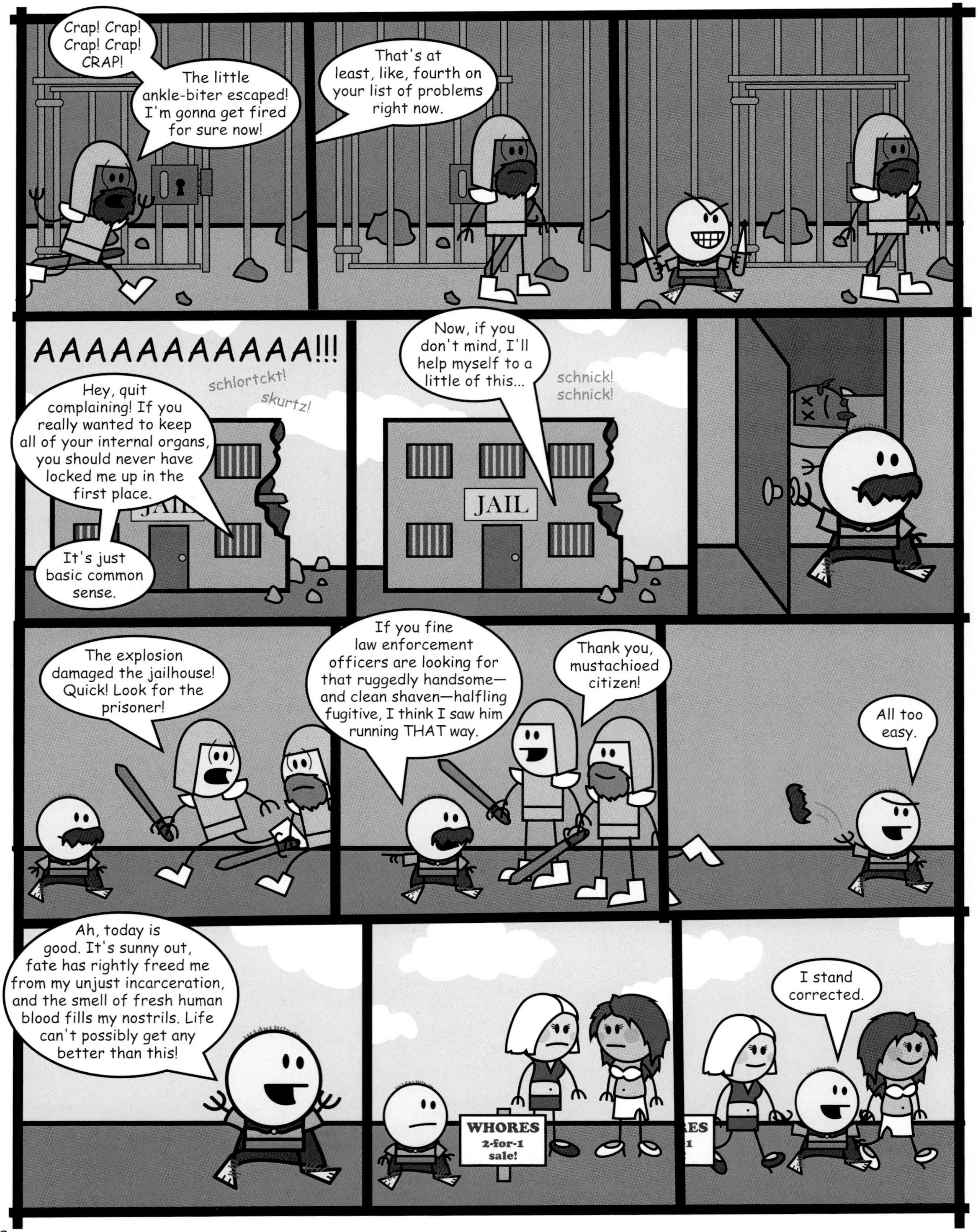

Crap! Crap! Crap! Crap! CRAP!
The little ankle-biter escaped! I'm gonna get fired for sure now!
That's at least, like, fourth on your list of problems right now.
AAAAAAAAAAA!!!
schlortckt!
skurtz!
Hey, quit complaining! If you really wanted to keep all of your internal organs, you should never have locked me up in the first place.
It's just basic common sense.
JAIL
Now, if you don't mind, I'll help myself to a little of this...
schnick! schnick!
JAIL
The explosion damaged the jailhouse! Quick! Look for the prisoner!
If you fine law enforcement officers are looking for that ruggedly handsome—and clean shaven—halfling fugitive, I think I saw him running THAT way.
Thank you, mustachioed citizen!
All too easy.
Ah, today is good. It's sunny out, fate has rightly freed me from my unjust incarceration, and the smell of fresh human blood fills my nostrils. Life can't possibly get any better than this!
WHORES 2-for-1 sale!
I stand corrected.

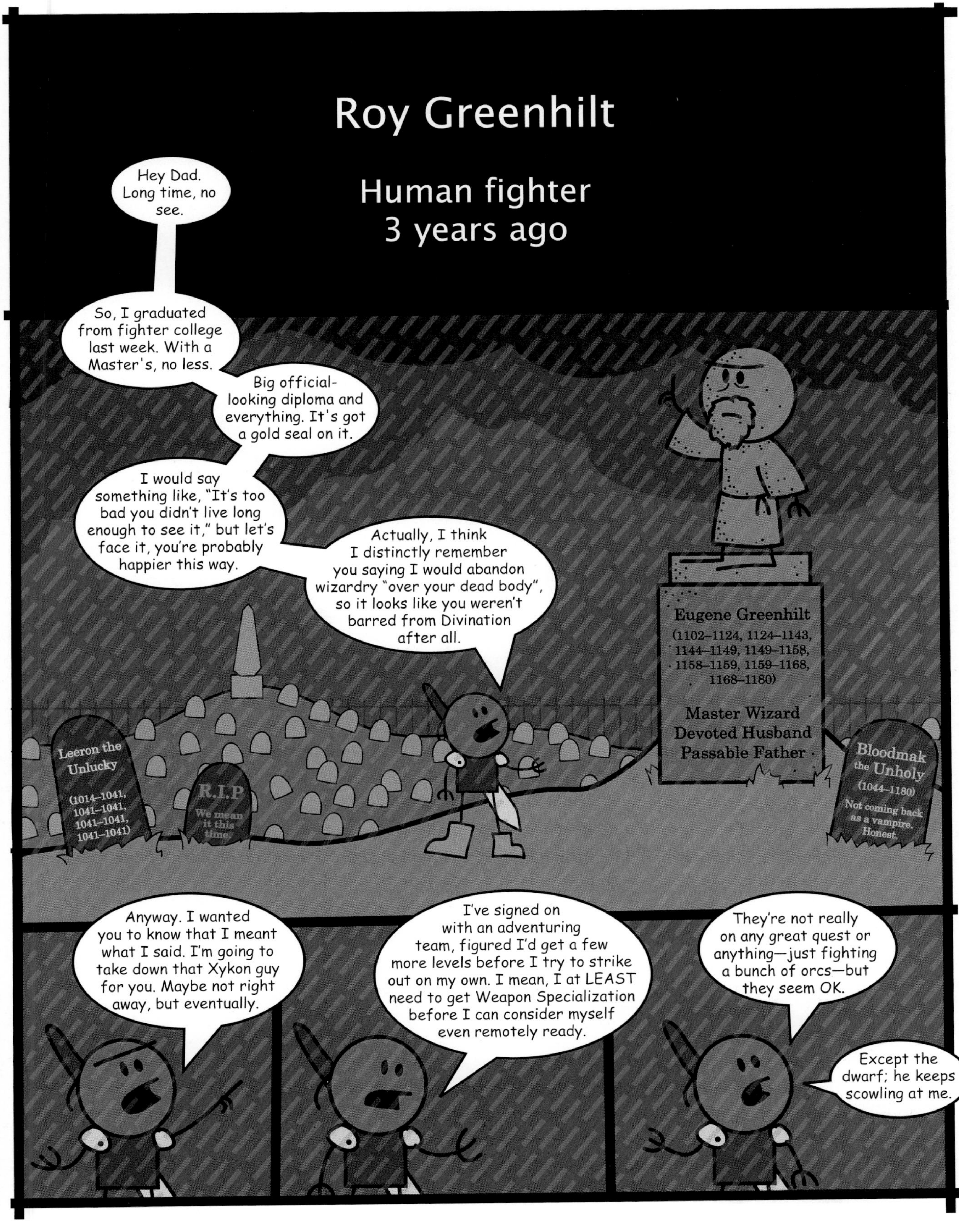
Roy Greenhilt
Human fighter
3 years ago
Hey Dad. Long time, no see.
So, I graduated from fighter college last week. With a Master's, no less.
Big official-looking diploma and everything. It's got a gold seal on it.
I would say something like, "It's too bad you didn't live long enough to see it," but let's face it, you're probably happier this way.
Actually, I think I distinctly remember you saying I would abandon wizardry "over your dead body", so it looks like you weren't barred from Divination after all.
Leeron the Unlucky (1014–1041, 1041–1041, 1041–1041, 1041–1041)
R.I.P We mean it this time.
Eugene Greenhilt (1102–1124, 1124–1143, 1144–1149, 1149–1158, 1158–1159, 1159–1168, 1168–1180)
Master Wizard Devoted Husband Passable Father
Bloodmak the Unholy (1044–1180) Not coming back as a vampire. Honest.
Anyway. I wanted you to know that I meant what I said. I'm going to take down that Xykon guy for you. Maybe not right away, but eventually.
I've signed on with an adventuring team, figured I'd get a few more levels before I try to strike out on my own. I mean, I at LEAST need to get Weapon Specialization before I can consider myself even remotely ready.
They're not really on any great quest or anything—just fighting a bunch of orcs—but they seem OK.
Except the dwarf; he keeps scowling at me.

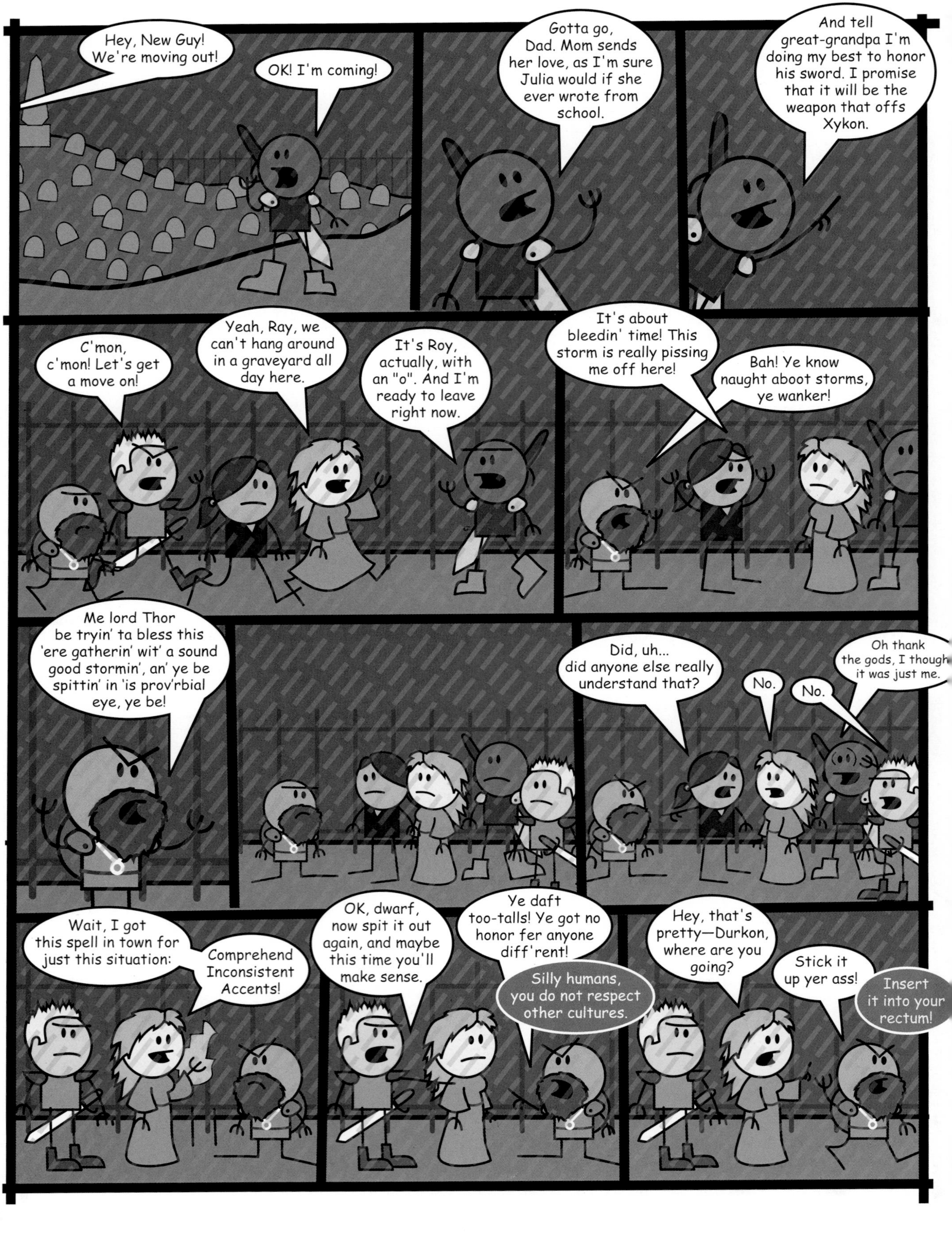
Hey, New Guy! We're moving out!
OK! I'm coming!
Gotta go, Dad. Mom sends her love, as I'm sure Julia would if she ever wrote from school.
And tell great-grandpa I'm doing my best to honor his sword. I promise that it will be the weapon that offs Xykon.
C'mon, c'mon! Let's get a move on!
Yeah, Ray, we can't hang around in a graveyard all day here.
It's Roy, actually, with an "o". And I'm ready to leave right now.
It's about bleedin' time! This storm is really pissing me off here!
Bah! Ye know naught aboot storms, ye wanker!
Me lord Thor be tryin' ta bless this 'ere gatherin' wit' a sound good stormin', an' ye be spittin' in 'is prov'rbial eye, ye be!
Did, uh... did anyone else really understand that?
No.
No.
Oh thank the gods, I though it was just me.
Wait, I got this spell in town for just this situation:
Comprehend Inconsistent Accents!
OK, dwarf, now spit it out again, and maybe this time you'll make sense.
Ye daft too-talls! Ye got no honor fer anyone diff'rent!
Silly humans, you do not respect other cultures.
Hey, that's pretty—Durkon, where are you going?
Stick it up yer ass!
Insert it into your rectum!

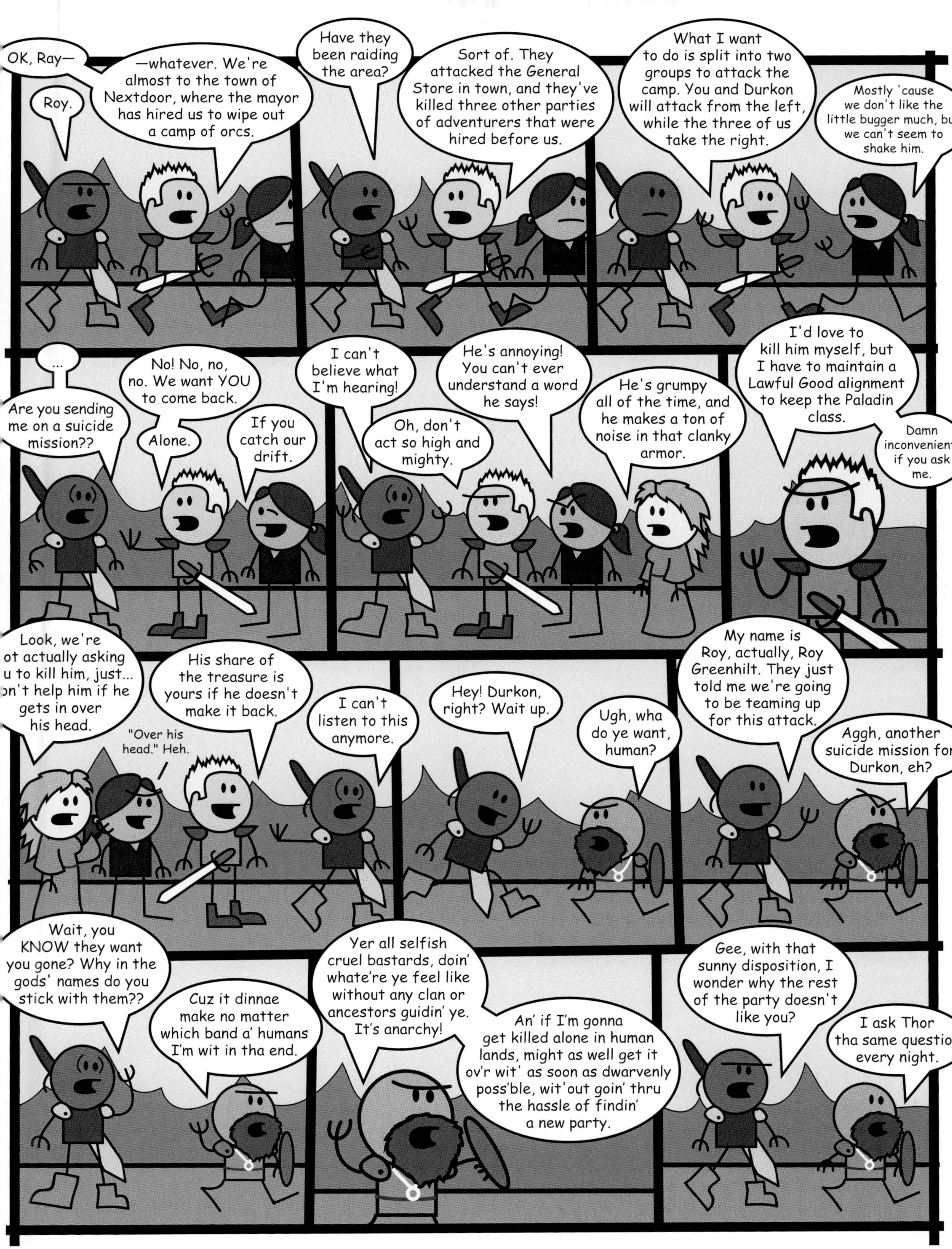
OK, Ray—
—whatever. We're almost to the town of Nextdoor, where the mayor has hired us to wipe out a camp of orcs.
Roy.
Have they been raiding the area?
Sort of. They attacked the General Store in town, and they've killed three other parties of adventurers that were hired before us.
What I want to do is split into two groups to attack the camp. You and Durkon will attack from the left, while the three of us take the right.
Mostly 'cause we don't like the little bugger much, but we can't seem to shake him.
...
Are you sending me on a suicide mission??
No! No, no, no. We want YOU to come back.
Alone.
If you catch our drift.
I can't believe what I'm hearing!
He's annoying! You can't ever understand a word he says!
Oh, don't act so high and mighty.
He's grumpy all of the time, and he makes a ton of noise in that clanky armor.
I'd love to kill him myself, but I have to maintain a Lawful Good alignment to keep the Paladin class.
Damn inconvenient, if you ask me.
Look, we're ot actually asking u to kill him, just... on't help him if he gets in over his head.
His share of the treasure is yours if he doesn't make it back.
"Over his head." Heh.
I can't listen to this anymore.
Hey! Durkon, right? Wait up.
Ugh, wha do ye want, human?
My name is Roy, actually, Roy Greenhilt. They just told me we're going to be teaming up for this attack.
Aggh, another suicide mission for Durkon, eh?
Wait, you KNOW they want you gone? Why in the gods' names do you stick with them??
Cuz it dinnae make no matter which band a' humans I'm wit in tha end.
Yer all selfish cruel bastards, doin' whate're ye feel like without any clan or ancestors guidin' ye. It's anarchy!
An' if I'm gonna get killed alone in human lands, might as well get it ov'r wit' as soon as dwarvenly poss'ble, wit'out goin' thru the hassle of findin' a new party.
Gee, with that sunny disposition, I wonder why the rest of the party doesn't like you?
I ask Thor tha same question every night.

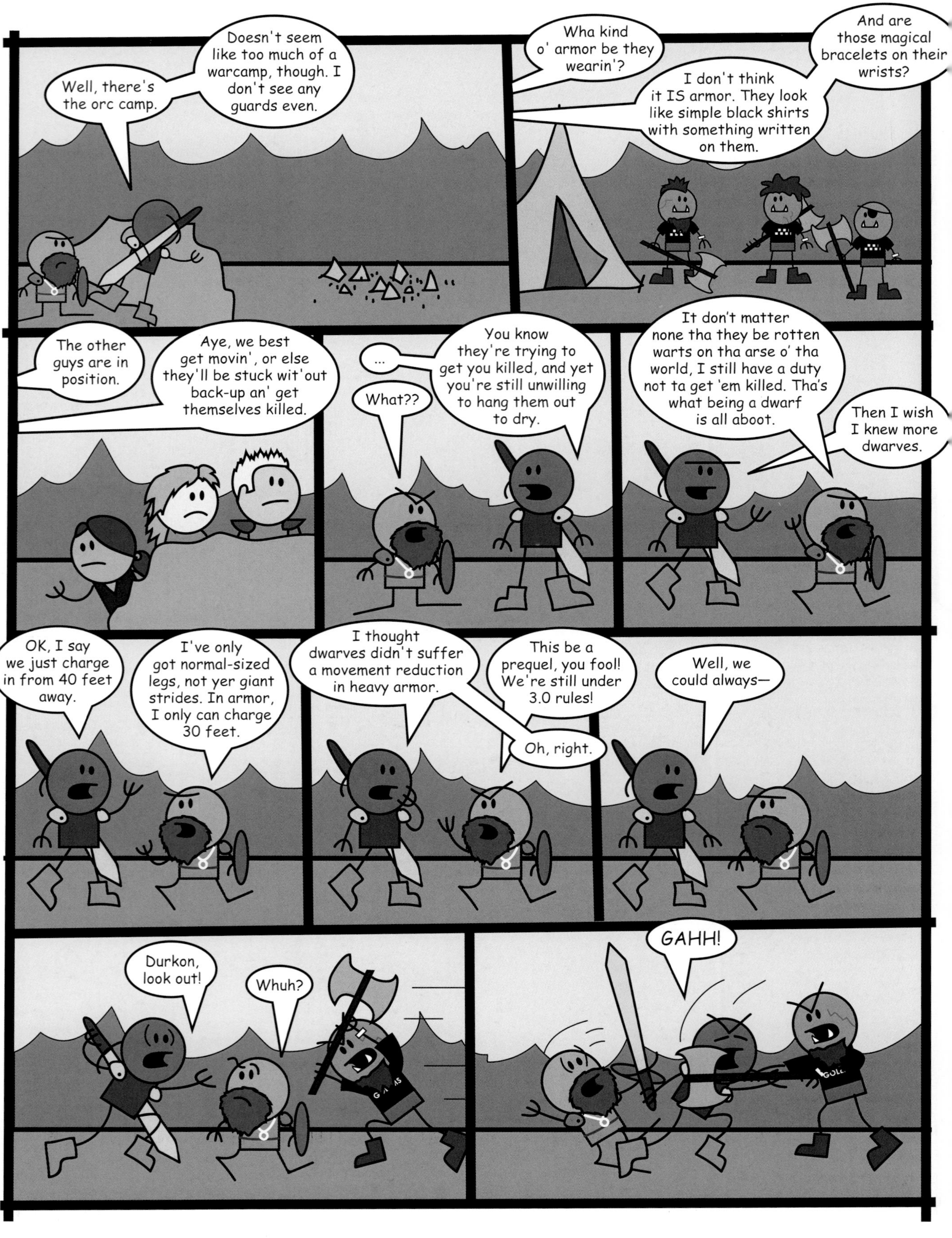
Well, there's the orc camp.
Doesn't seem like too much of a warcamp, though. I don't see any guards even.
Wha kind o' armor be they wearin'?
I don't think it IS armor. They look like simple black shirts with something written on them.
And are those magical bracelets on their wrists?
The other guys are in position.
Aye, we best get movin', or else they'll be stuck wit'out back-up an' get themselves killed.
...
You know they're trying to get you killed, and yet you're still unwilling to hang them out to dry.
What??
It don't matter none tha they be rotten warts on tha arse o' tha world, I still have a duty not ta get 'em killed. Tha's what being a dwarf is all aboot.
Then I wish I knew more dwarves.
OK, I say we just charge in from 40 feet away.
I've only got normal-sized legs, not yer giant strides. In armor, I only can charge 30 feet.
I thought dwarves didn't suffer a movement reduction in heavy armor.
This be a prequel, you fool! We're still under 3.0 rules!
Oh, right.
Well, we could always—
Durkon, look out!
Whuh?
GAHH!

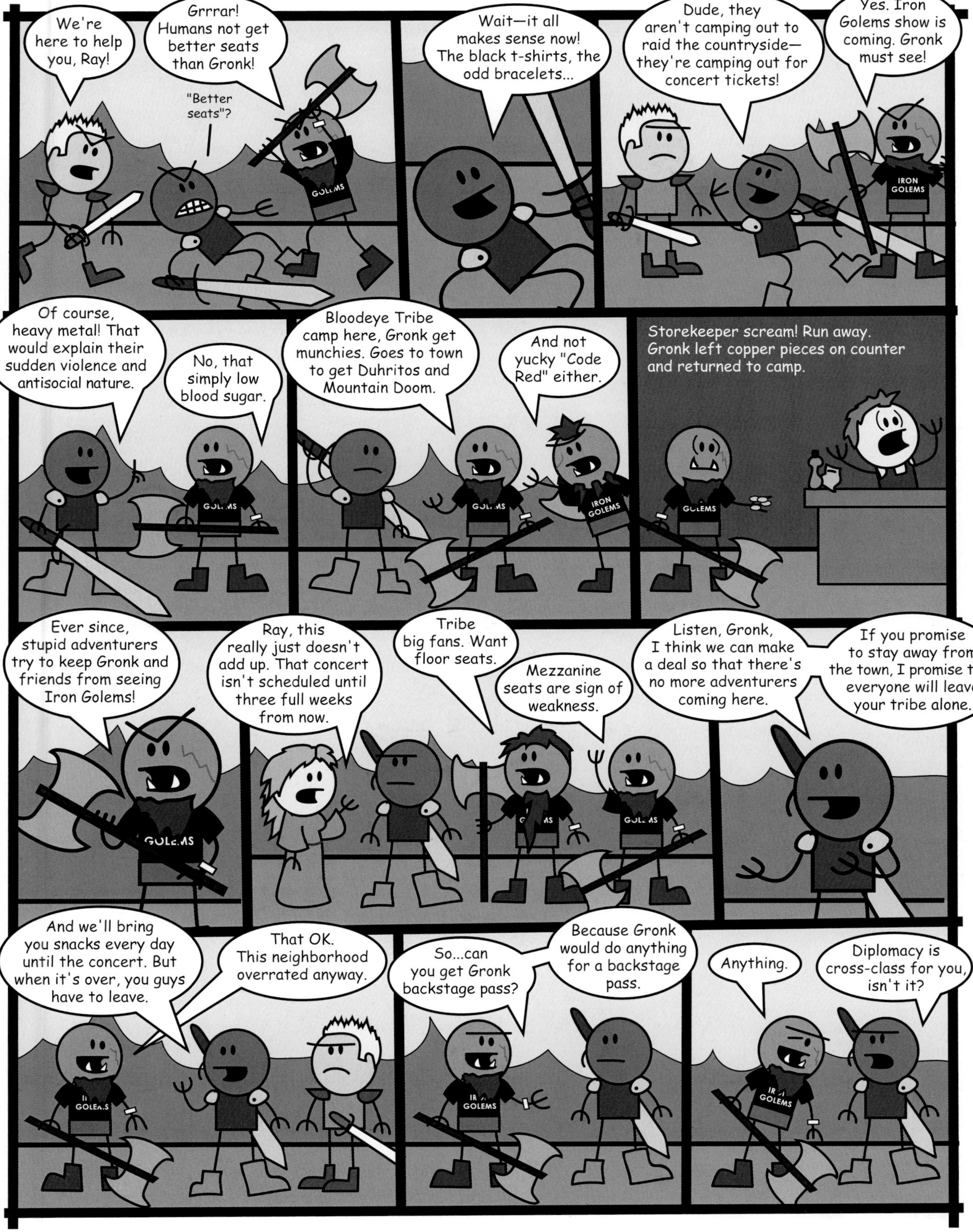
We're here to help you, Ray!
Grrrar! Humans not get better seats than Gronk!
"Better seats"?
GOLEMS
Wait—it all makes sense now! The black t-shirts, the odd bracelets...
Dude, they aren't camping out to raid the countryside—they're camping out for concert tickets!
Yes. Iron Golems show is coming. Gronk must see!
IRON GOLEMS
Of course, heavy metal! That would explain their sudden violence and antisocial nature.
No, that simply low blood sugar.
Bloodeye Tribe camp here, Gronk get munchies. Goes to town to get Duhritos and Mountain Doom.
And not yucky "Code Red" either.
IRON GOLEMS
Storekeeper scream! Run away. Gronk left copper pieces on counter and returned to camp.
Ever since, stupid adventurers try to keep Gronk and friends from seeing Iron Golems!
Ray, this really just doesn't add up. That concert isn't scheduled until three full weeks from now.
Tribe big fans. Want floor seats.
Mezzanine seats are sign of weakness.
Listen, Gronk, I think we can make a deal so that there's no more adventurers coming here.
If you promise to stay away from the town, I promise that everyone will leave your tribe alone.
And we'll bring you snacks every day until the concert. But when it's over, you guys have to leave.
That OK. This neighborhood overrated anyway.
So...can you get Gronk backstage pass?
Because Gronk would do anything for a backstage pass.
Anything.
Diplomacy is cross-class for you, isn't it?
GOLEMS

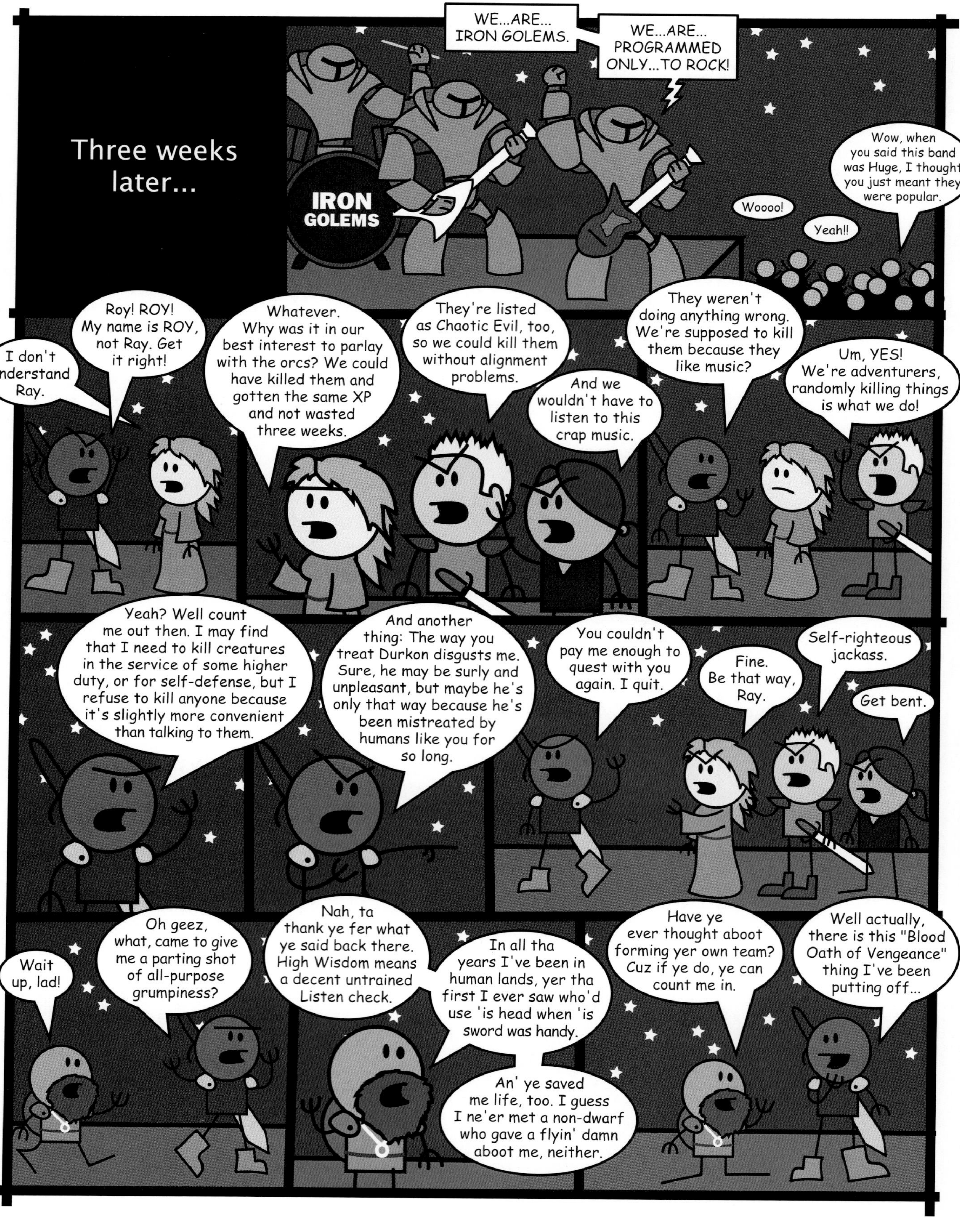
Three weeks later...
WE...ARE... IRON GOLEMS.
WE...ARE... PROGRAMMED ONLY...TO ROCK!
IRON GOLEMS
Woooo!
Yeah!!
Wow, when you said this band was Huge, I thought you just meant they were popular.
I don't understand Ray.
Roy! ROY! My name is ROY, not Ray. Get it right!
Whatever. Why was it in our best interest to parlay with the orcs? We could have killed them and gotten the same XP and not wasted three weeks.
They're listed as Chaotic Evil, too, so we could kill them without alignment problems.
And we wouldn't have to listen to this crap music.
They weren't doing anything wrong. We're supposed to kill them because they like music?
Um, YES! We're adventurers, randomly killing things is what we do!
Yeah? Well count me out then. I may find that I need to kill creatures in the service of some higher duty, or for self-defense, but I refuse to kill anyone because it's slightly more convenient than talking to them.
And another thing: The way you treat Durkon disgusts me. Sure, he may be surly and unpleasant, but maybe he's only that way because he's been mistreated by humans like you for so long.
You couldn't pay me enough to quest with you again. I quit.
Fine. Be that way, Ray.
Self-righteous jackass.
Get bent.
Wait up, lad!
Oh geez, what, came to give me a parting shot of all-purpose grumpiness?
Nah, ta thank ye fer what ye said back there. High Wisdom means a decent untrained Listen check.
In all tha years I've been in human lands, yer tha first I ever saw who'd use 'is head when 'is sword was handy.
An' ye saved me life, too. I guess I ne'er met a non-dwarf who gave a flyin' damn aboot me, neither.
Have ye ever thought aboot forming yer own team? Cuz if ye do, ye can count me in.
Well actually, there is this "Blood Oath of Vengeance" thing I've been putting off...

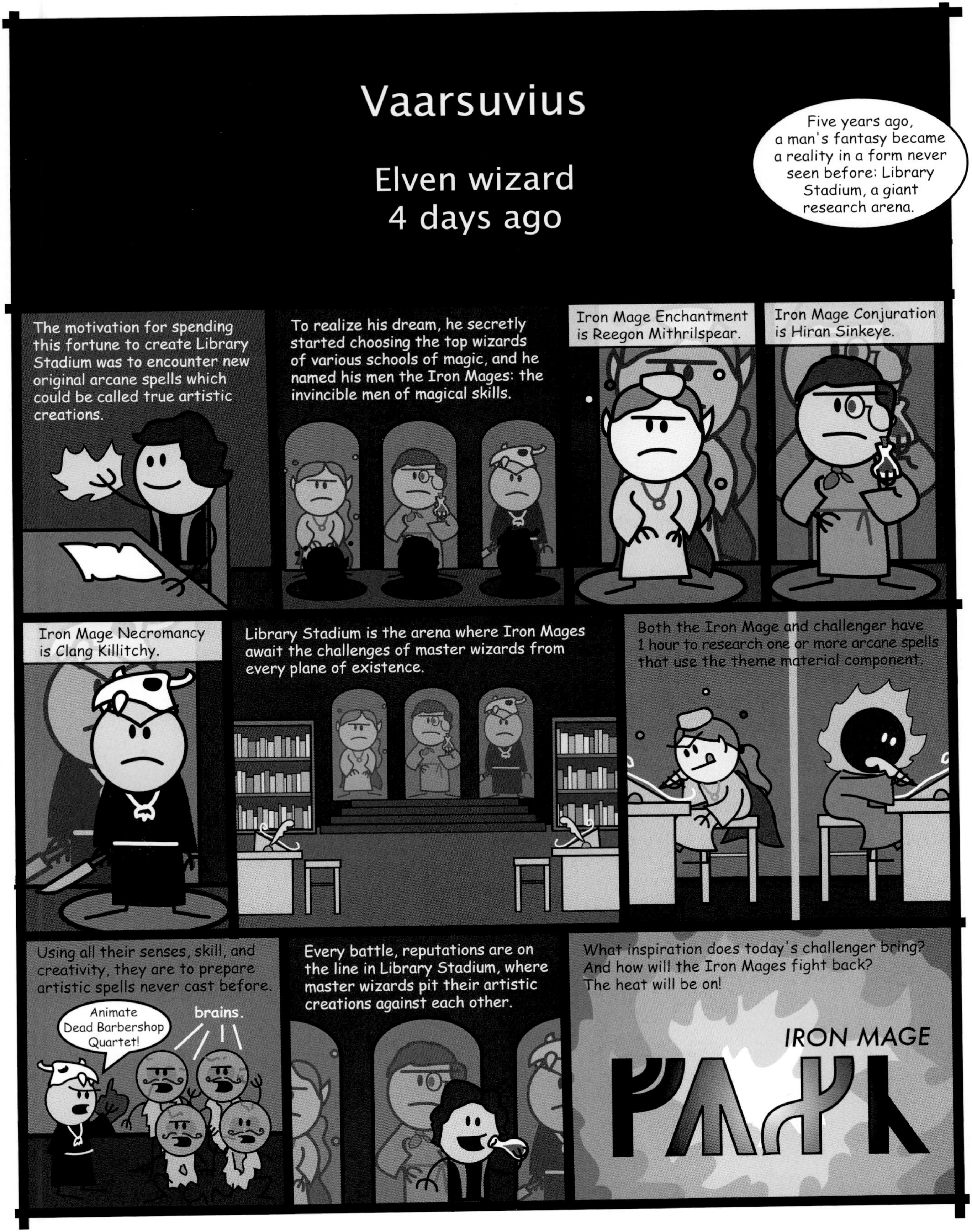
Vaarsuvius
Elven wizard
4 days ago
Five years ago, a man's fantasy became a reality in a form never seen before: Library Stadium, a giant research arena.
The motivation for spending this fortune to create Library Stadium was to encounter new original arcane spells which could be called true artistic creations.
To realize his dream, he secretly started choosing the top wizards of various schools of magic, and he named his men the Iron Mages: the invincible men of magical skills.
Iron Mage Enchantment is Reegon Mithrilspear.
Iron Mage Conjuration is Hiran Sinkeye.
Iron Mage Necromancy is Clang Killitchy.
Library Stadium is the arena where Iron Mages await the challenges of master wizards from every plane of existence.
Both the Iron Mage and challenger have 1 hour to research one or more arcane spells that use the theme material component.
Using all their senses, skill, and creativity, they are to prepare artistic spells never cast before.
Animate Dead Barbershop Quartet!
brains.
Every battle, reputations are on the line in Library Stadium, where master wizards pit their artistic creations against each other.
What inspiration does today's challenger bring? And how will the Iron Mages fight back? The heat will be on!
IRON MAGE

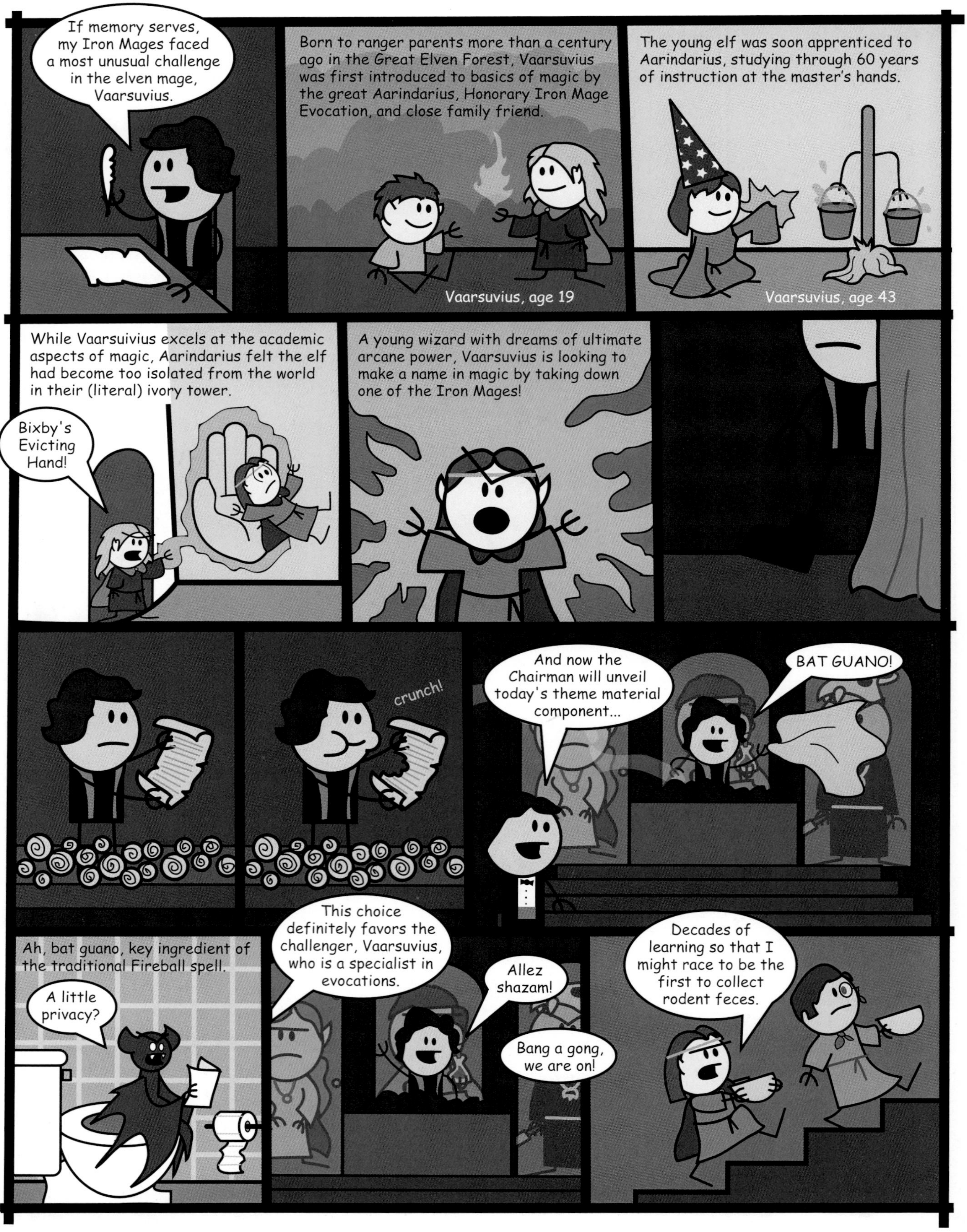

If memory serves, my Iron Mages faced a most unusual challenge in the elven mage, Vaarsuvius.
Born to ranger parents more than a century ago in the Great Elven Forest, Vaarsuvius was first introduced to basics of magic by the great Aarindarius, Honorary Iron Mage Evocation, and close family friend.
Vaarsuvius, age 19
The young elf was soon apprenticed to Aarindarius, studying through 60 years of instruction at the master's hands.
Vaarsuvius, age 43
While Vaarsuivius excels at the academic aspects of magic, Aarindarius felt the elf had become too isolated from the world in their (literal) ivory tower.
Bixby's Evicting Hand!
A young wizard with dreams of ultimate arcane power, Vaarsuvius is looking to make a name in magic by taking down one of the Iron Mages!
crunch!
And now the Chairman will unveil today's theme material component...
BAT GUANO!
Ah, bat guano, key ingredient of the traditional Fireball spell.
A little privacy?
This choice definitely favors the challenger, Vaarsuvius, who is a specialist in evocations.
Allez shazam!
Bang a gong, we are on!
Decades of learning so that I might race to be the first to collect rodent feces.

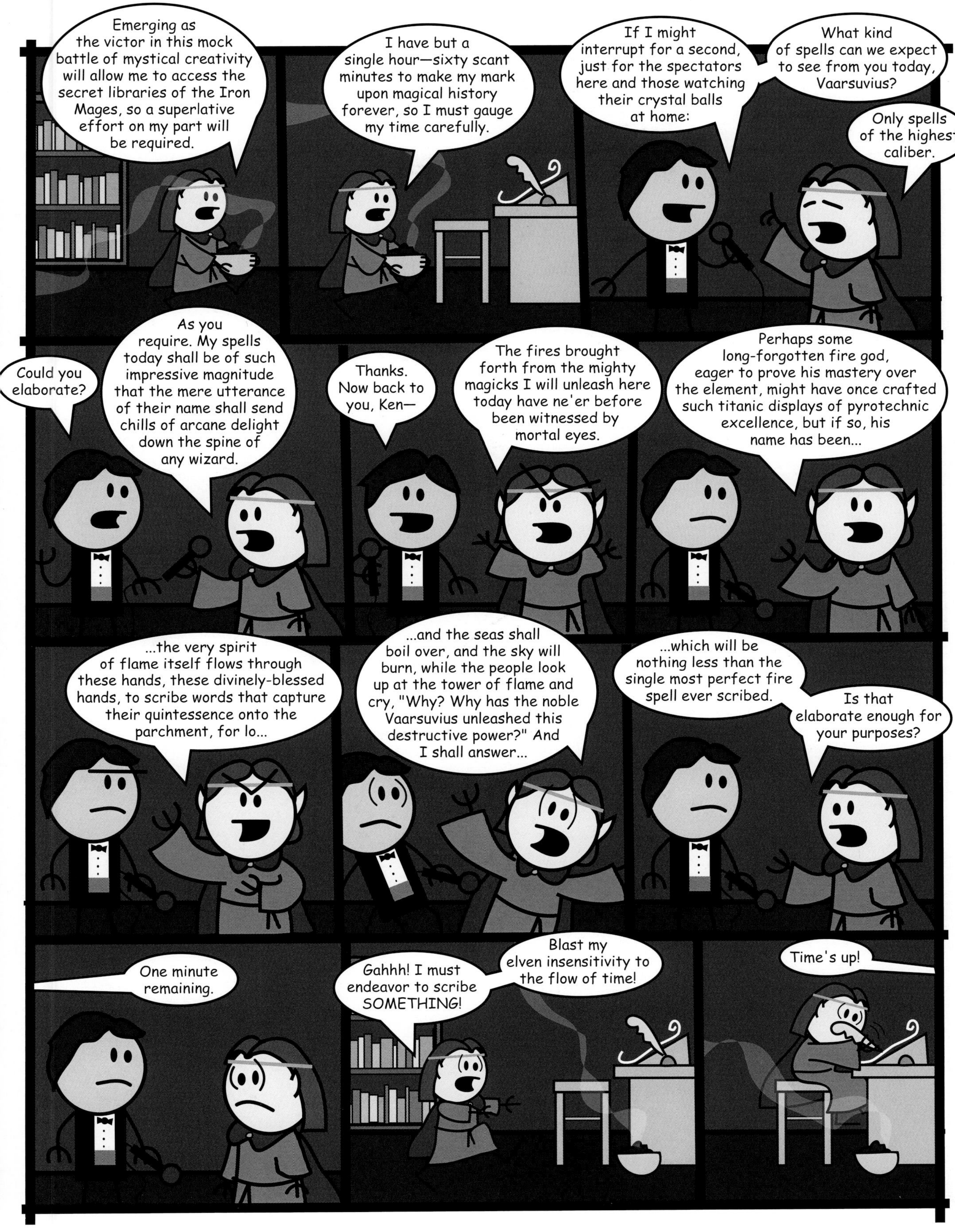
Emerging as the victor in this mock battle of mystical creativity will allow me to access the secret libraries of the Iron Mages, so a superlative effort on my part will be required.
I have but a single hour—sixty scant minutes to make my mark upon magical history forever, so I must gauge my time carefully.
If I might interrupt for a second, just for the spectators here and those watching their crystal balls at home:
What kind of spells can we expect to see from you today, Vaarsuvius?
Only spells of the highest caliber.
Could you elaborate?
As you require. My spells today shall be of such impressive magnitude that the mere utterance of their name shall send chills of arcane delight down the spine of any wizard.
Thanks. Now back to you, Ken—
The fires brought forth from the mighty magicks I will unleash here today have ne'er before been witnessed by mortal eyes.
Perhaps some long-forgotten fire god, eager to prove his mastery over the element, might have once crafted such titanic displays of pyrotechnic excellence, but if so, his name has been...
...the very spirit of flame itself flows through these hands, these divinely-blessed hands, to scribe words that capture their quintessence onto the parchment, for lo...
...and the seas shall boil over, and the sky will burn, while the people look up at the tower of flame and cry, "Why? Why has the noble Vaarsuvius unleashed this destructive power?" And I shall answer...
...which will be nothing less than the single most perfect fire spell ever scribed.
Is that elaborate enough for your purposes?
One minute remaining.
Gahhh! I must endeavor to scribe SOMETHING!
Blast my elven insensitivity to the flow of time!
Time's up!

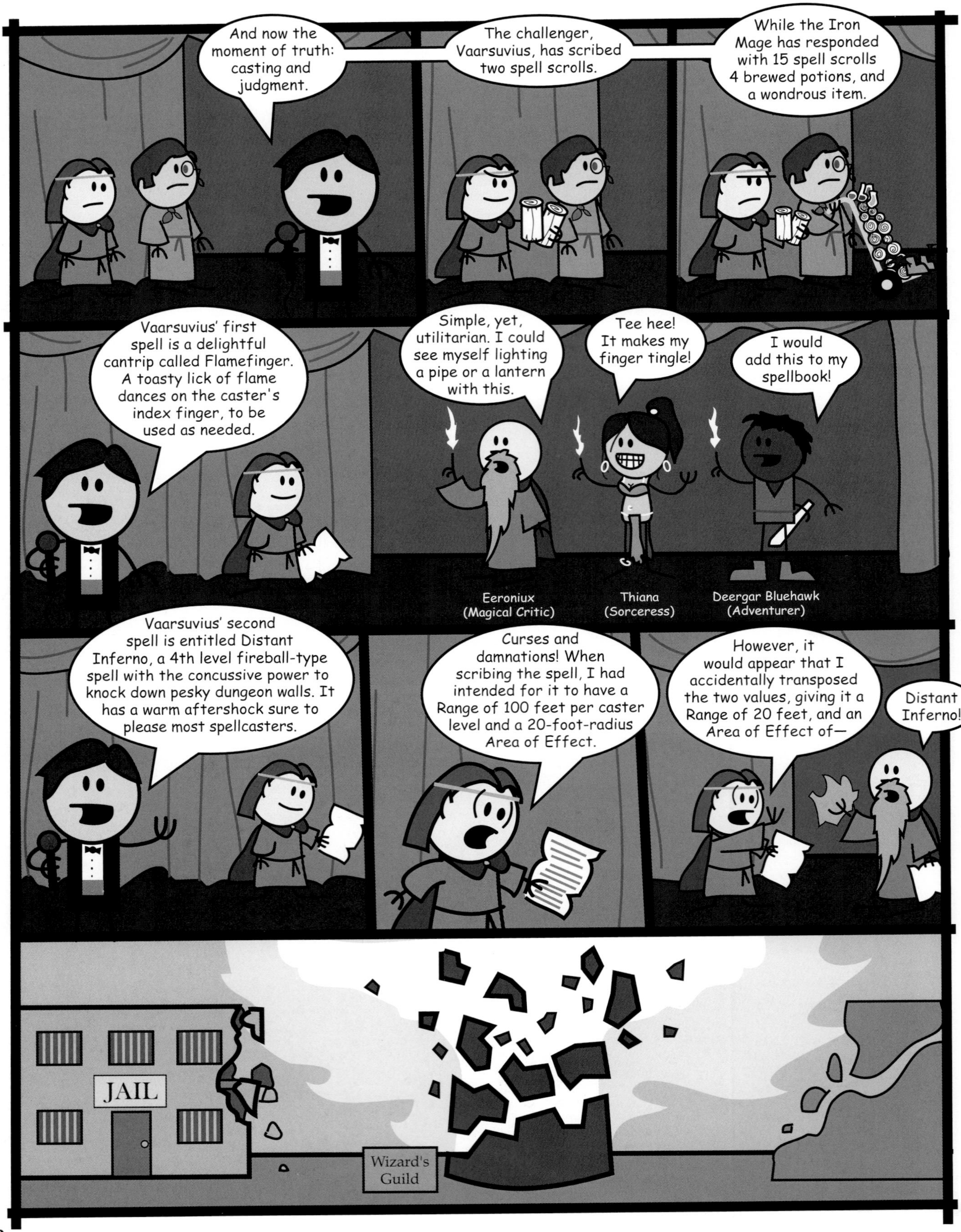
And now the moment of truth: casting and judgment.
The challenger, Vaarsuvius, has scribed two spell scrolls.
While the Iron Mage has responded with 15 spell scrolls 4 brewed potions, and a wondrous item.
Vaarsuvius' first spell is a delightful cantrip called Flamefinger. A toasty lick of flame dances on the caster's index finger, to be used as needed.
Simple, yet, utilitarian. I could see myself lighting a pipe or a lantern with this.
Tee hee! It makes my finger tingle!
I would add this to my spellbook!
Eeroniux (Magical Critic)
Thiana (Sorceress)
Deergar Bluehawk (Adventurer)
Vaarsuvius' second spell is entitled Distant Inferno, a 4th level fireball-type spell with the concussive power to knock down pesky dungeon walls. It has a warm aftershock sure to please most spellcasters.
Curses and damnations! When scribing the spell, I had intended for it to have a Range of 100 feet per caster level and a 20-foot-radius Area of Effect.
However, it would appear that I accidentally transposed the two values, giving it a Range of 20 feet, and an Area of Effect of—
Distant Inferno!
JAIL
Wizard's Guild

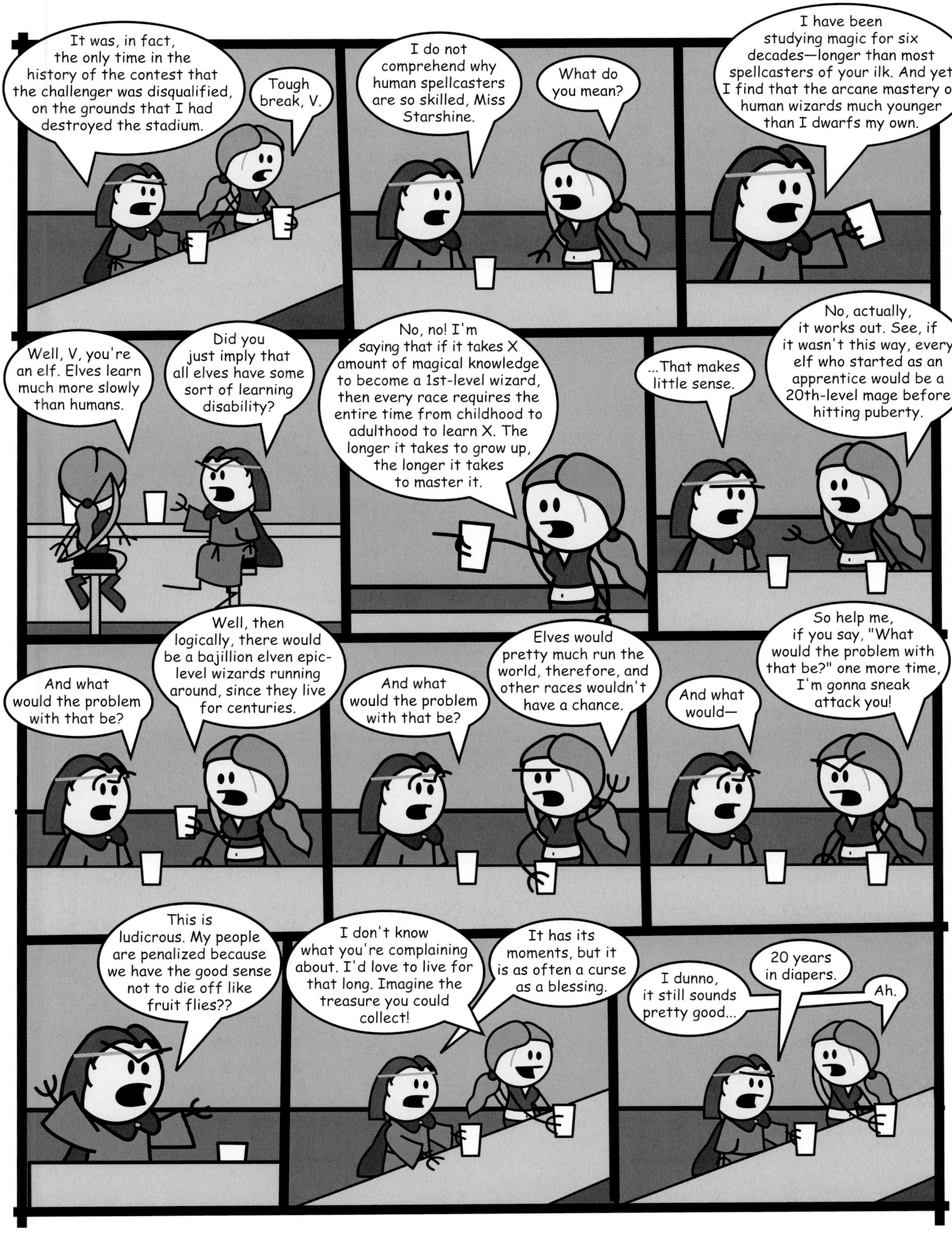
It was, in fact, the only time in the history of the contest that the challenger was disqualified, on the grounds that I had destroyed the stadium.
Tough break, V.
I do not comprehend why human spellcasters are so skilled, Miss Starshine.
What do you mean?
I have been studying magic for six decades—longer than most spellcasters of your ilk. And yet, I find that the arcane mastery of human wizards much younger than I dwarfs my own.
Well, V, you're an elf. Elves learn much more slowly than humans.
Did you just imply that all elves have some sort of learning disability?
No, no! I'm saying that if it takes X amount of magical knowledge to become a 1st-level wizard, then every race requires the entire time from childhood to adulthood to learn X. The longer it takes to grow up, the longer it takes to master it.
...That makes little sense.
No, actually, it works out. See, if it wasn't this way, every elf who started as an apprentice would be a 20th-level mage before hitting puberty.
And what would the problem with that be?
Well, then logically, there would be a bajillion elven epic-level wizards running around, since they live for centuries.
And what would the problem with that be?
Elves would pretty much run the world, therefore, and other races wouldn't have a chance.
And what would—
So help me, if you say, "What would the problem with that be?" one more time, I'm gonna sneak attack you!
This is ludicrous. My people are penalized because we have the good sense not to die off like fruit flies??
I don't know what you're complaining about. I'd love to live for that long. Imagine the treasure you could collect!
It has its moments, but it is as often a curse as a blessing.
I dunno, it still sounds pretty good...
20 years in diapers.
Ah.

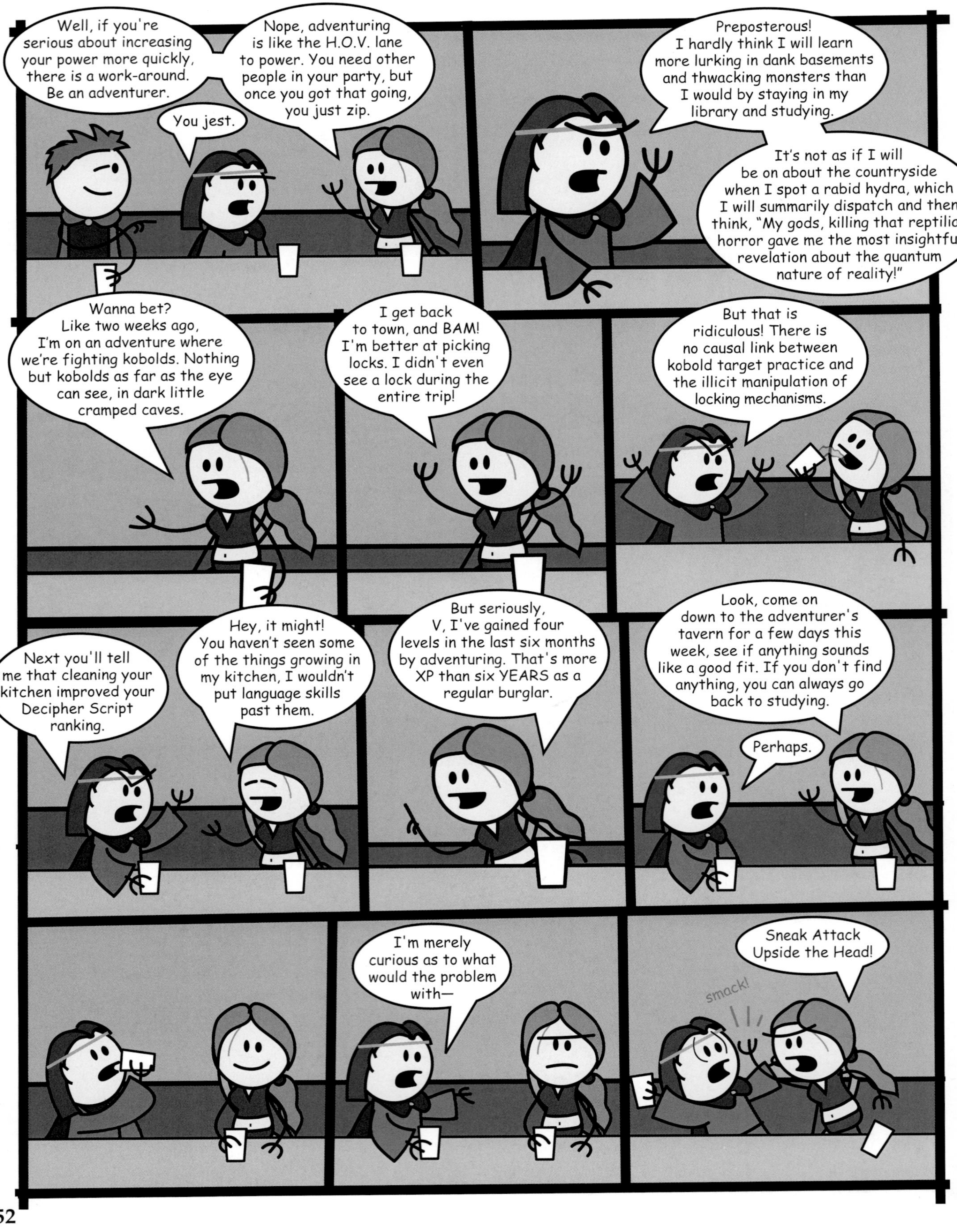
Well, if you're serious about increasing your power more quickly, there is a work-around. Be an adventurer.
You jest.
Nope, adventuring is like the H.O.V. lane to power. You need other people in your party, but once you got that going, you just zip.
Preposterous! I hardly think I will learn more lurking in dank basements and thwacking monsters than I would by staying in my library and studying.
It's not as if I will be on about the countryside when I spot a rabid hydra, which I will summarily dispatch and then think, "My gods, killing that reptilian horror gave me the most insightful revelation about the quantum nature of reality!"
Wanna bet? Like two weeks ago, I'm on an adventure where we're fighting kobolds. Nothing but kobolds as far as the eye can see, in dark little cramped caves.
I get back to town, and BAM! I'm better at picking locks. I didn't even see a lock during the entire trip!
But that is ridiculous! There is no causal link between kobold target practice and the illicit manipulation of locking mechanisms.
Next you'll tell me that cleaning your kitchen improved your Decipher Script ranking.
Hey, it might! You haven't seen some of the things growing in my kitchen, I wouldn't put language skills past them.
But seriously, V, I've gained four levels in the last six months by adventuring. That's more XP than six YEARS as a regular burglar.
Look, come on down to the adventurer's tavern for a few days this week, see if anything sounds like a good fit. If you don't find anything, you can always go back to studying.
Perhaps.
I'm merely curious as to what would the problem with—
smack!
Sneak Attack Upside the Head!

The Day Before Yesterday

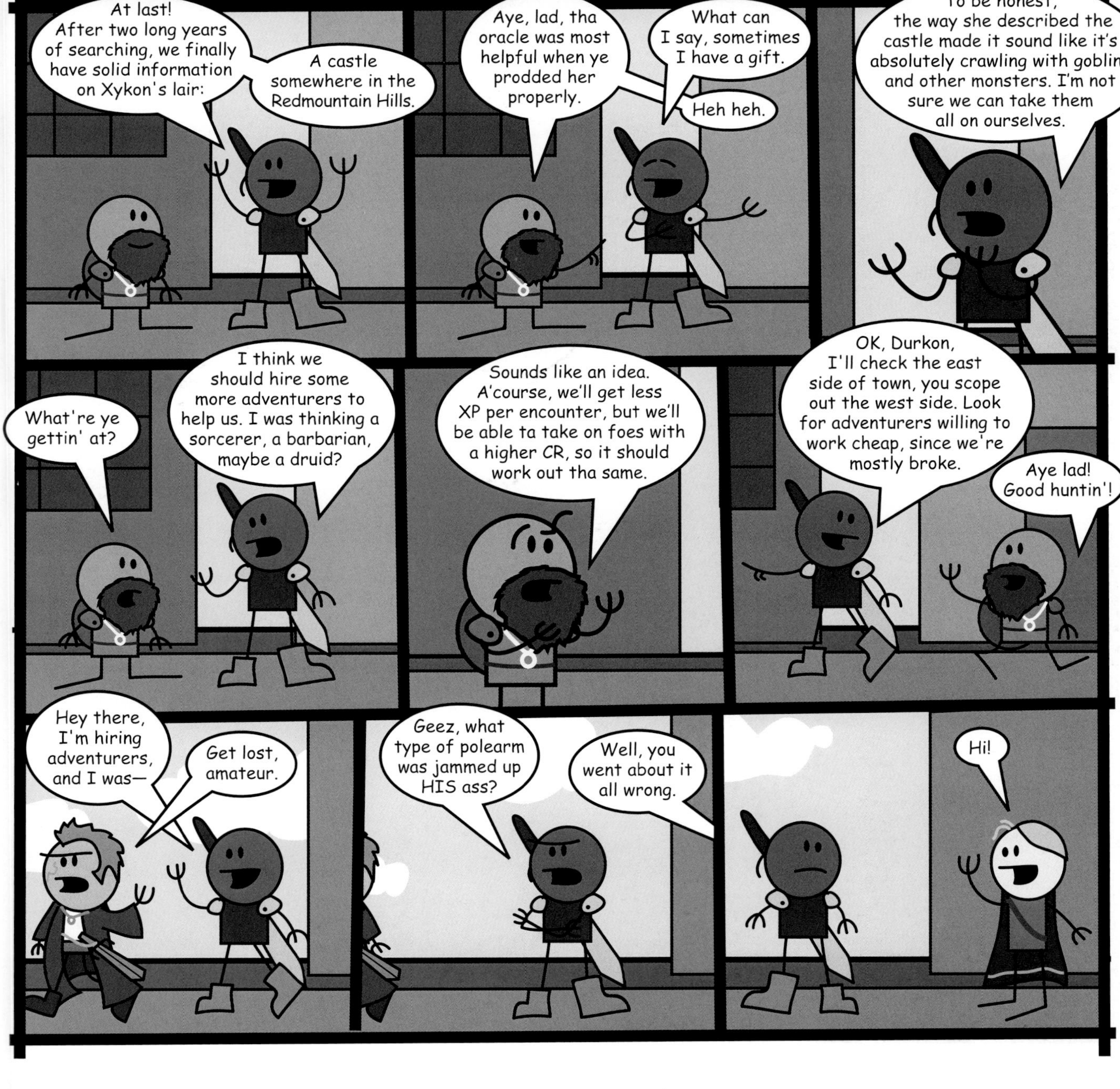

At last! After two long years of searching, we finally have solid information on Xykon's lair:
A castle somewhere in the Redmountain Hills.
Aye, lad, tha oracle was most helpful when ye prodded her properly.
What can I say, sometimes I have a gift.
Heh heh.
To be honest, the way she described the castle made it sound like it's absolutely crawling with goblins and other monsters. I'm not sure we can take them all on ourselves.
What're ye gettin' at?
I think we should hire some more adventurers to help us. I was thinking a sorcerer, a barbarian, maybe a druid?
Sounds like an idea. A'course, we'll get less XP per encounter, but we'll be able ta take on foes with a higher CR, so it should work out tha same.
OK, Durkon, I'll check the east side of town, you scope out the west side. Look for adventurers willing to work cheap, since we're mostly broke.
Aye lad! Good huntin'!
Hey there, I'm hiring adventurers, and I was—
Get lost, amateur.
Geez, what type of polearm was jammed up HIS ass?
Well, you went about it all wrong.
Hi!

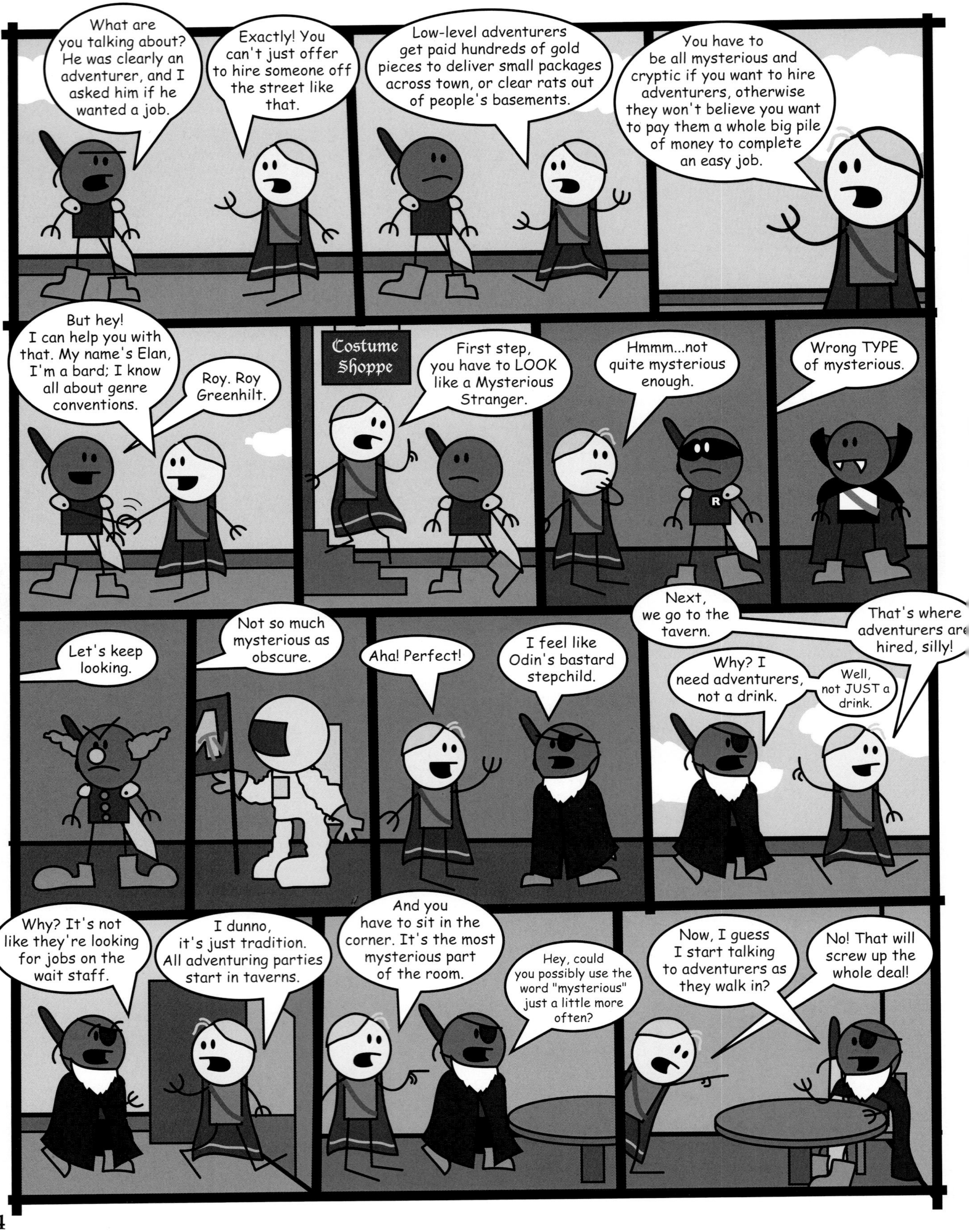
What are you talking about? He was clearly an adventurer, and I asked him if he wanted a job.
Exactly! You can't just offer to hire someone off the street like that.
Low-level adventurers get paid hundreds of gold pieces to deliver small packages across town, or clear rats out of people's basements.
You have to be all mysterious and cryptic if you want to hire adventurers, otherwise they won't believe you want to pay them a whole big pile of money to complete an easy job.
But hey! I can help you with that. My name's Elan, I'm a bard; I know all about genre conventions.
Roy. Roy Greenhilt.
Costume Shoppe
First step, you have to LOOK like a Mysterious Stranger.
Hmmm...not quite mysterious enough.
Wrong TYPE of mysterious.
Let's keep looking.
Not so much mysterious as obscure.
Aha! Perfect!
I feel like Odin's bastard stepchild.
Next, we go to the tavern.
That's where adventurers are hired, silly!
Why? I need adventurers, not a drink.
Well, not JUST a drink.
Why? It's not like they're looking for jobs on the wait staff.
I dunno, it's just tradition. All adventuring parties start in taverns.
And you have to sit in the corner. It's the most mysterious part of the room.
Hey, could you possibly use the word "mysterious" just a little more often?
Now, I guess I start talking to adventurers as they walk in?
No! That will screw up the whole deal!

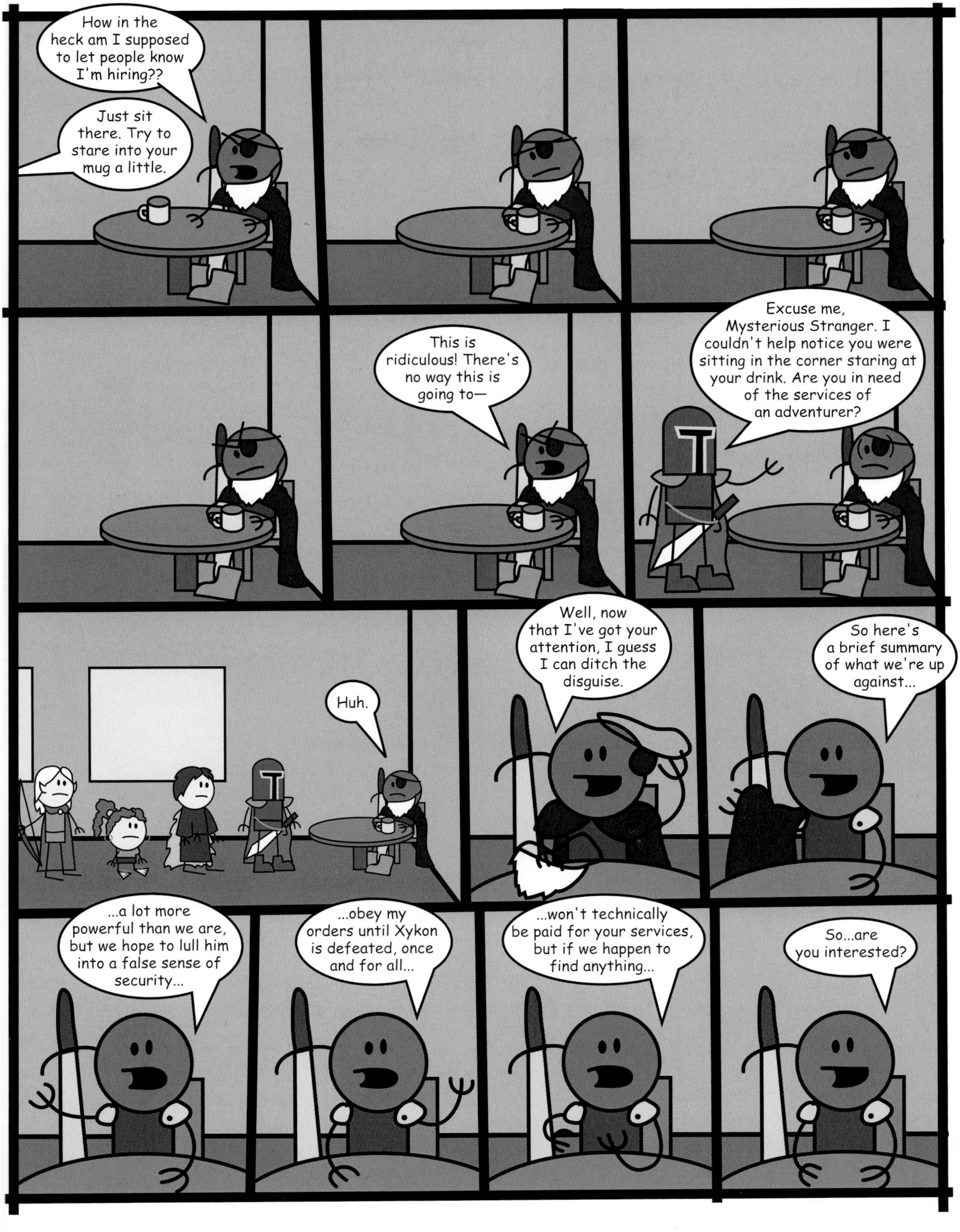
How in the heck am I supposed to let people know I'm hiring??
Just sit there. Try to stare into your mug a little.
This is ridiculous! There's no way this is going to—
Excuse me, Mysterious Stranger. I couldn't help notice you were sitting in the corner staring at your drink. Are you in need of the services of an adventurer?
Huh.
Well, now that I've got your attention, I guess I can ditch the disguise.
So here's a brief summary of what we're up against...
...a lot more powerful than we are, but we hope to lull him into a false sense of security...
...obey my orders until Xykon is defeated, once and for all...
...won't technically be paid for your services, but if we happen to find anything...
So...are you interested?

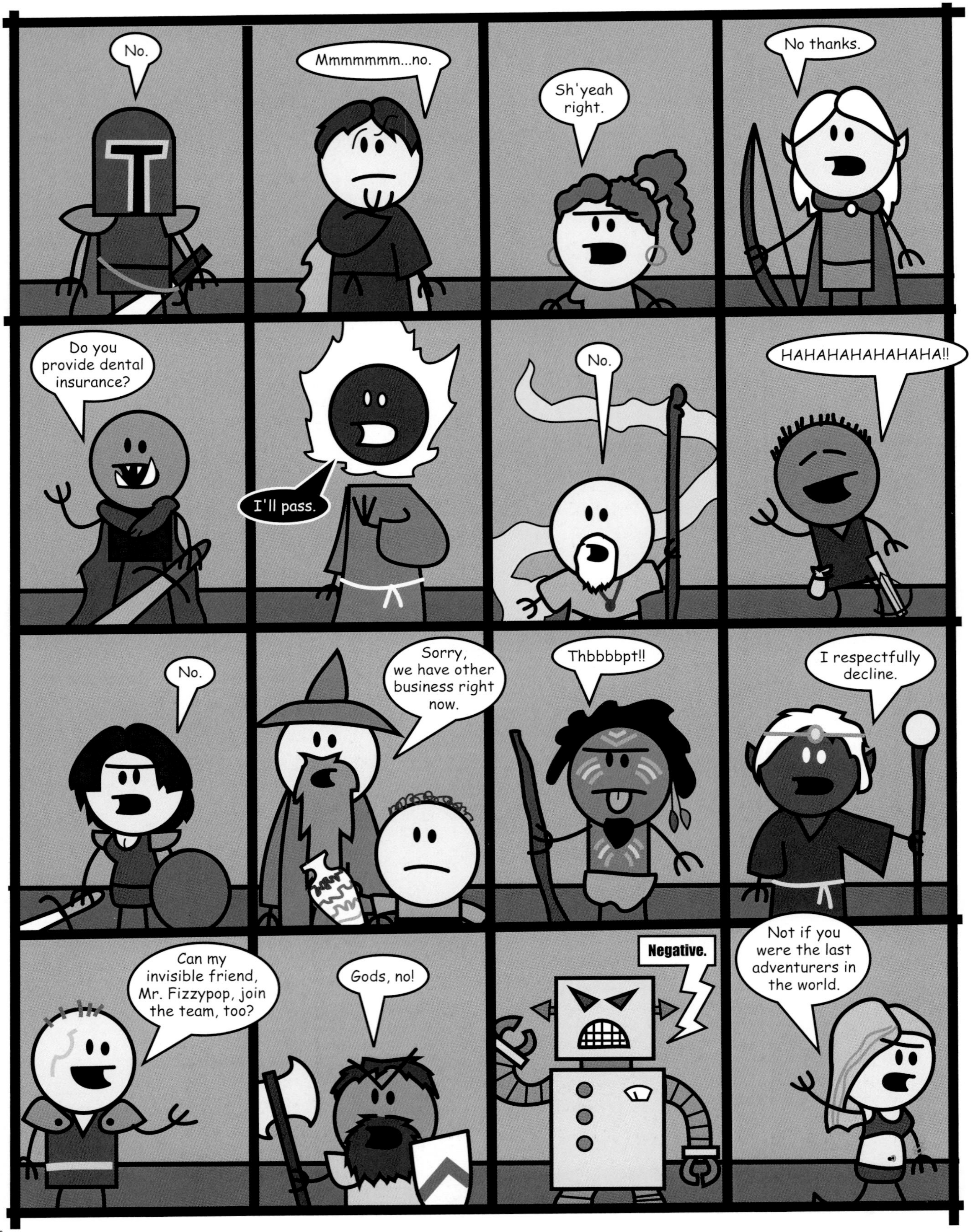
No.
Mmmmmmm...no.
Sh'yeah right.
No thanks.
Do you provide dental insurance?
I'll pass.
No.
HAHAHAHAHAHAHA!!
No.
Sorry, we have other business right now.
Thbbbbpt!!
I respectfully decline.
Can my invisible friend, Mr. Fizzypop, join the team, too?
Gods, no!
Negative.
Not if you were the last adventurers in the world.

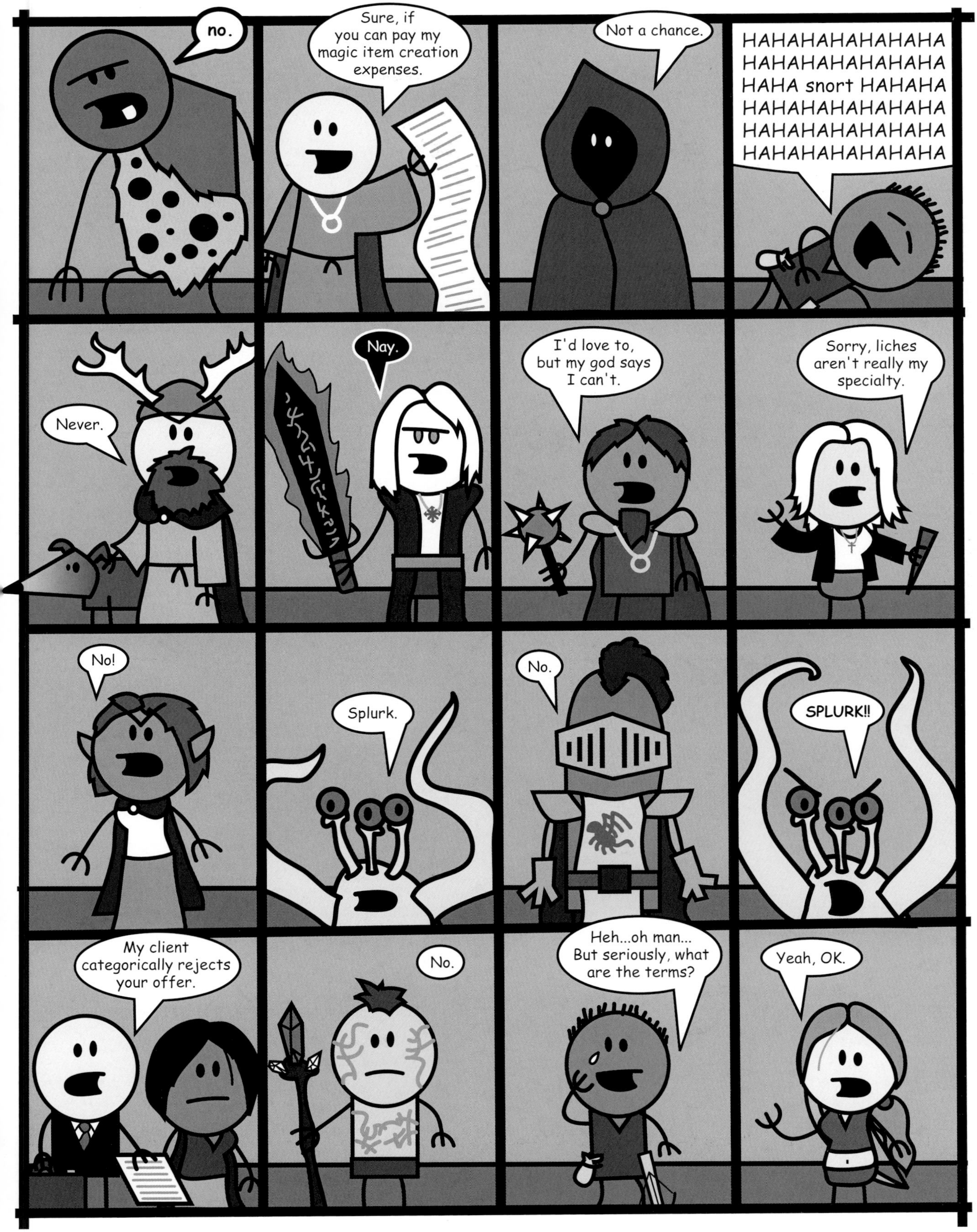
no.
Sure, if you can pay my magic item creation expenses.
Not a chance.
HAHAHAHAHAHAHA HAHAHAHAHAHAHA HAHA snort HAHAHA HAHAHAHAHAHAHA HAHAHAHAHAHAHA HAHAHAHAHAHAHA
Never.
Nay.
I'd love to, but my god says I can't.
Sorry, liches aren't really my specialty.
No!
Splurk.
No.
SPLURK!!
My client categorically rejects your offer.
No.
Heh...oh man... But seriously, what are the terms?
Yeah, OK.

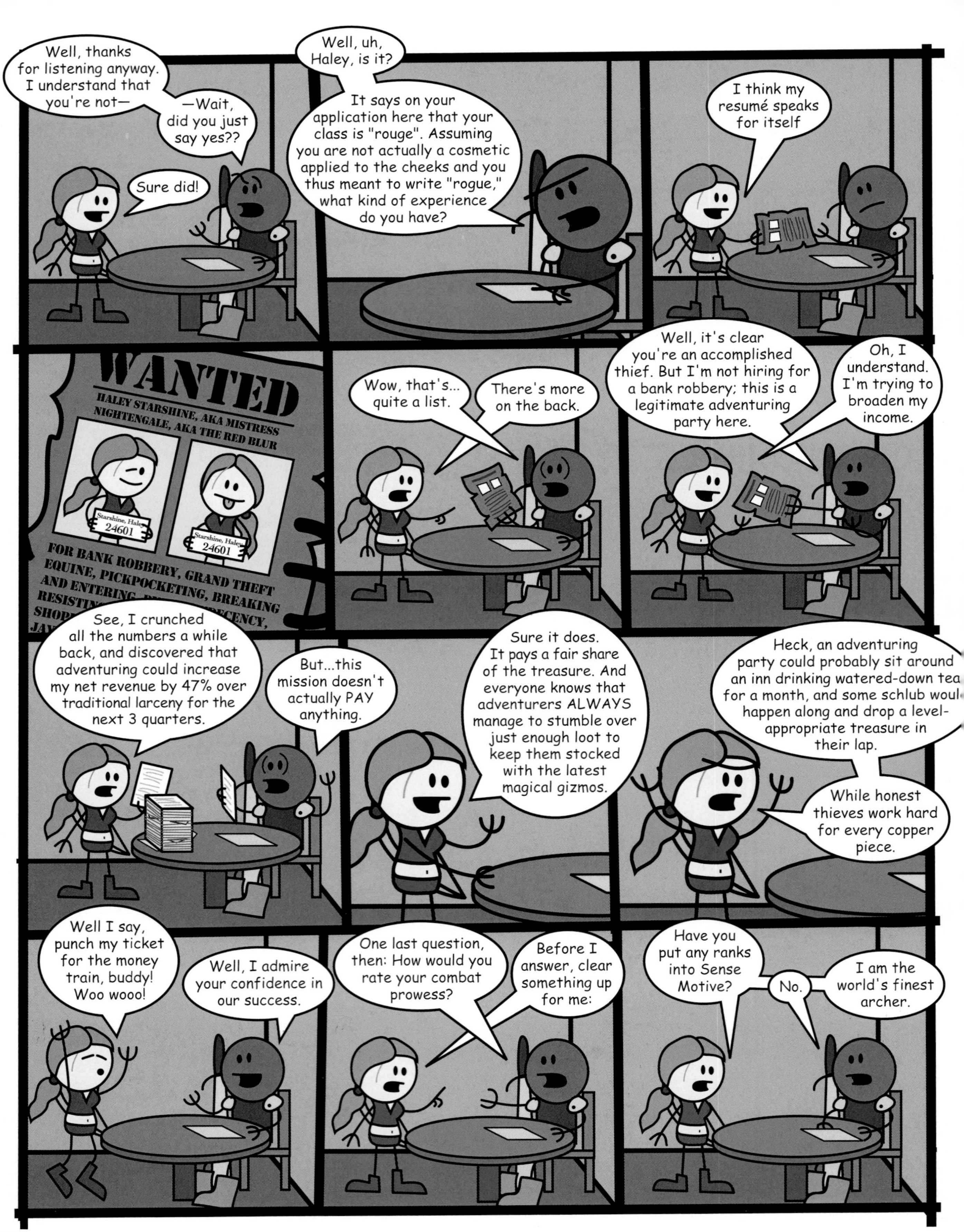
Well, thanks for listening anyway. I understand that you're not—
—Wait, did you just say yes??
Sure did!
Well, uh, Haley, is it?
It says on your application here that your class is "rouge". Assuming you are not actually a cosmetic applied to the cheeks and you thus meant to write "rogue," what kind of experience do you have?
I think my resumé speaks for itself
WANTED
HALEY STARSHINE, AKA MISTRESS NIGHTENGALE, AKA THE RED BLUR
Starshine, Haley 24601
Starshine, Haley 24601
FOR BANK ROBBERY, GRAND THEFT EQUINE, PICKPOCKETING, BREAKING AND ENTERING,
Wow, that's... quite a list.
There's more on the back.
Well, it's clear you're an accomplished thief. But I'm not hiring for a bank robbery; this is a legitimate adventuring party here.
Oh, I understand. I'm trying to broaden my income.
See, I crunched all the numbers a while back, and discovered that adventuring could increase my net revenue by 47% over traditional larceny for the next 3 quarters.
But...this mission doesn't actually PAY anything.
Sure it does. It pays a fair share of the treasure. And everyone knows that adventurers ALWAYS manage to stumble over just enough loot to keep them stocked with the latest magical gizmos.
Heck, an adventuring party could probably sit around an inn drinking watered-down tea for a month, and some schlub woul happen along and drop a level-appropriate treasure in their lap.
While honest thieves work hard for every copper piece.
Well I say, punch my ticket for the money train, buddy! Woo wooo!
Well, I admire your confidence in our success.
One last question, then: How would you rate your combat prowess?
Before I answer, clear something up for me:
Have you put any ranks into Sense Motive?
No.
I am the world's finest archer.

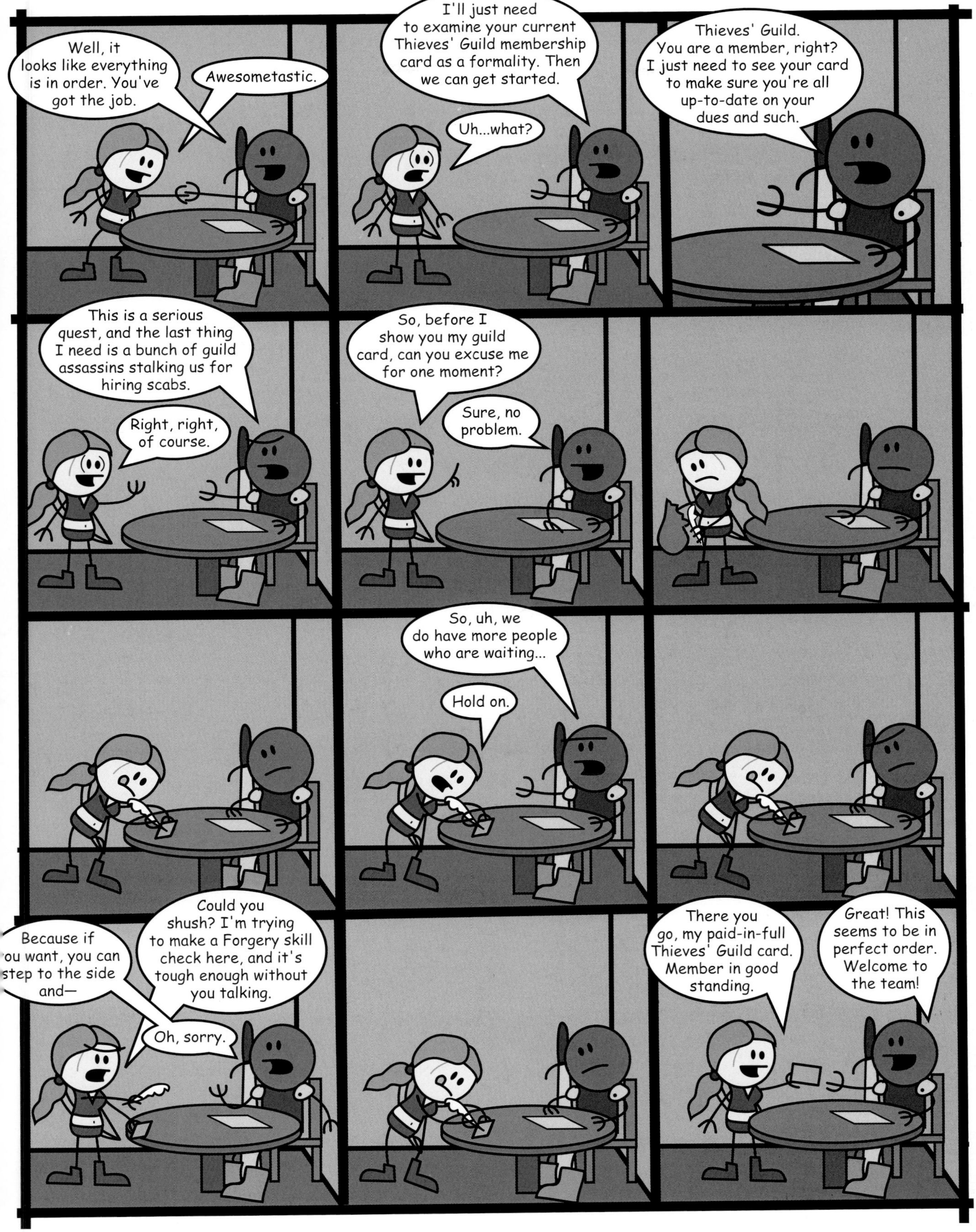

Well, it looks like everything is in order. You've got the job.
Awesometastic.
I'll just need to examine your current Thieves' Guild membership card as a formality. Then we can get started.
Uh...what?
Thieves' Guild. You are a member, right? I just need to see your card to make sure you're all up-to-date on your dues and such.
This is a serious quest, and the last thing I need is a bunch of guild assassins stalking us for hiring scabs.
Right, right, of course.
So, before I show you my guild card, can you excuse me for one moment?
Sure, no problem.
So, uh, we do have more people who are waiting...
Hold on.
Because if ou want, you can step to the side and—
Could you shush? I'm trying to make a Forgery skill check here, and it's tough enough without you talking.
Oh, sorry.
There you go, my paid-in-full Thieves' Guild card. Member in good standing.
Great! This seems to be in perfect order. Welcome to the team!

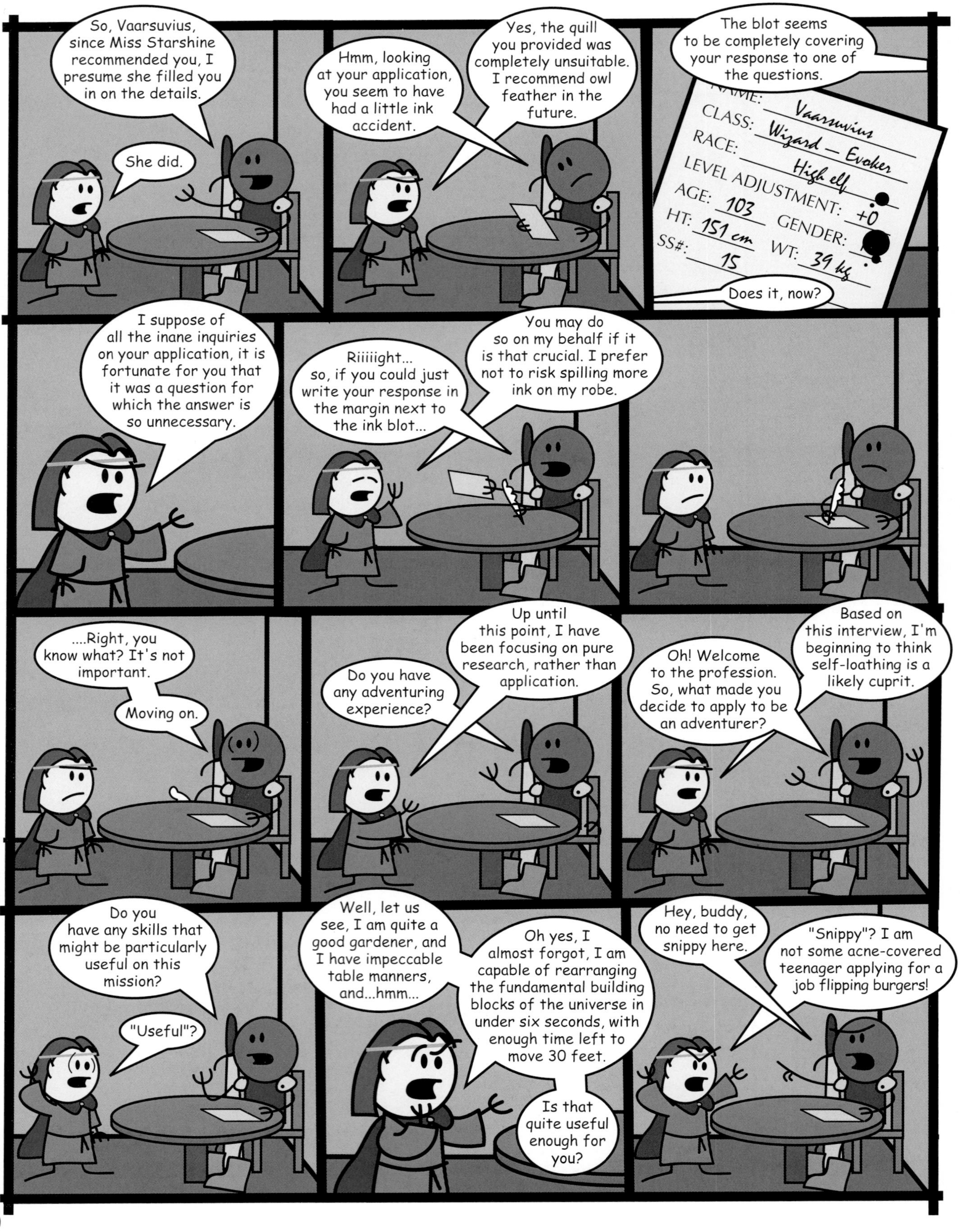
So, Vaarsuvius, since Miss Starshine recommended you, I presume she filled you in on the details.
She did.
Hmm, looking at your application, you seem to have had a little ink accident.
Yes, the quill you provided was completely unsuitable. I recommend owl feather in the future.
The blot seems to be completely covering your response to one of the questions.
CLASS: Wizard — Evoker
RACE: High elf
LEVEL ADJUSTMENT: +0
AGE: 103
GENDER:
HT: 151 cm
WT: 39 kg
SS#: 15
Does it, now?
I suppose of all the inane inquiries on your application, it is fortunate for you that it was a question for which the answer is so unnecessary.
Riiiiight... so, if you could just write your response in the margin next to the ink blot...
You may do so on my behalf if it is that crucial. I prefer not to risk spilling more ink on my robe.
....Right, you know what? It's not important.
Moving on.
Do you have any adventuring experience?
Up until this point, I have been focusing on pure research, rather than application.
Oh! Welcome to the profession. So, what made you decide to apply to be an adventurer?
Based on this interview, I'm beginning to think self-loathing is a likely cuprit.
Do you have any skills that might be particularly useful on this mission?
"Useful"?
Well, let us see, I am quite a good gardener, and I have impeccable table manners, and...hmm...
Oh yes, I almost forgot, I am capable of rearranging the fundamental building blocks of the universe in under six seconds, with enough time left to move 30 feet.
Is that quite useful enough for you?
Hey, buddy, no need to get snippy here.
"Snippy"? I am not some acne-covered teenager applying for a job flipping burgers!

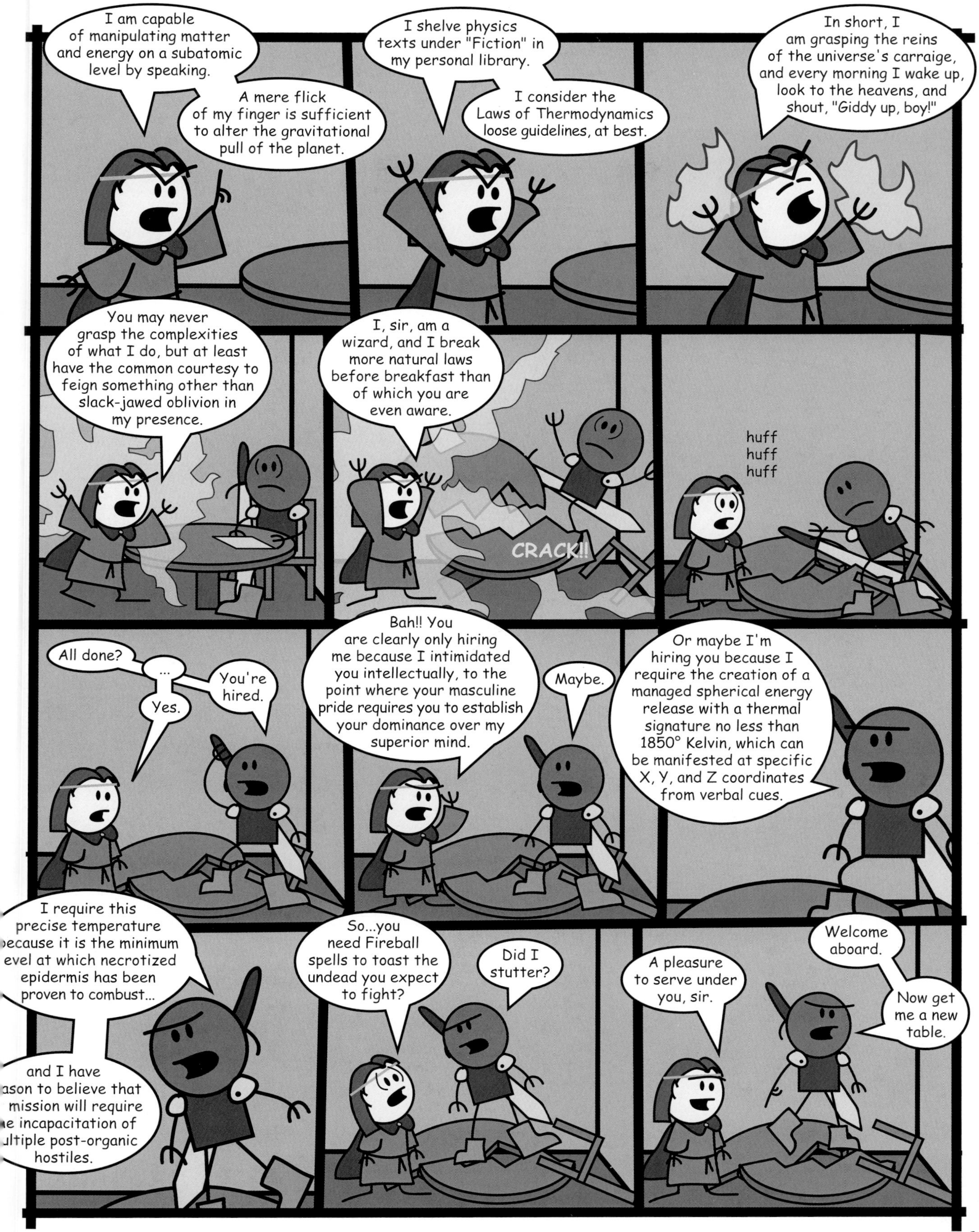

I am capable of manipulating matter and energy on a subatomic level by speaking.
A mere flick of my finger is sufficient to alter the gravitational pull of the planet.
I shelve physics texts under "Fiction" in my personal library.
I consider the Laws of Thermodynamics loose guidelines, at best.
In short, I am grasping the reins of the universe's carraige, and every morning I wake up, look to the heavens, and shout, "Giddy up, boy!"
You may never grasp the complexities of what I do, but at least have the common courtesy to feign something other than slack-jawed oblivion in my presence.
I, sir, am a wizard, and I break more natural laws before breakfast than of which you are even aware.
CRACK!!
huff huff huff
All done?
...
Yes.
You're hired.
Bah!! You are clearly only hiring me because I intimidated you intellectually, to the point where your masculine pride requires you to establish your dominance over my superior mind.
Maybe.
Or maybe I'm hiring you because I require the creation of a managed spherical energy release with a thermal signature no less than 1850° Kelvin, which can be manifested at specific X, Y, and Z coordinates from verbal cues.
I require this precise temperature ecause it is the minimum evel at which necrotized epidermis has been proven to combust...
and I have ason to believe that mission will require e incapacitation of ltiple post-organic hostiles.
So...you need Fireball spells to toast the undead you expect to fight?
Did I stutter?
A pleasure to serve under you, sir.
Welcome aboard.
Now get me a new table.

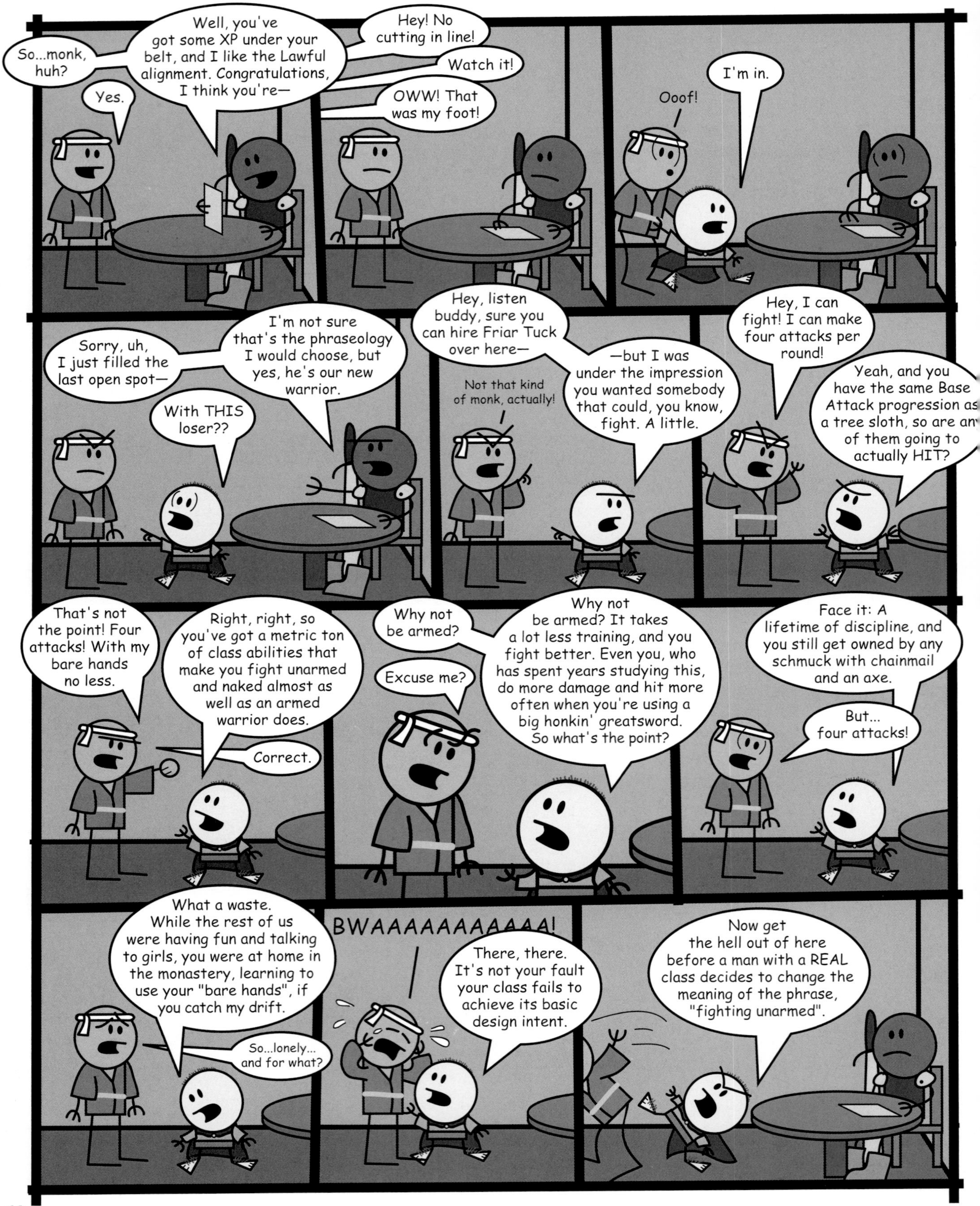
So...monk, huh?
Yes.
Well, you've got some XP under your belt, and I like the Lawful alignment. Congratulations, I think you're—
Hey! No cutting in line!
Watch it!
OWW! That was my foot!
Ooof!
I'm in.
Sorry, uh, I just filled the last open spot—
With THIS loser??
I'm not sure that's the phraseology I would choose, but yes, he's our new warrior.
Hey, listen buddy, sure you can hire Friar Tuck over here—
Not that kind of monk, actually!
—but I was under the impression you wanted somebody that could, you know, fight. A little.
Hey, I can fight! I can make four attacks per round!
Yeah, and you have the same Base Attack progression as a tree sloth, so are any of them going to actually HIT?
That's not the point! Four attacks! With my bare hands no less.
Right, right, so you've got a metric ton of class abilities that make you fight unarmed and naked almost as well as an armed warrior does.
Correct.
Why not be armed?
Excuse me?
Why not be armed? It takes a lot less training, and you fight better. Even you, who has spent years studying this, do more damage and hit more often when you're using a big honkin' greatsword. So what's the point?
Face it: A lifetime of discipline, and you still get owned by any schmuck with chainmail and an axe.
But... four attacks!
What a waste. While the rest of us were having fun and talking to girls, you were at home in the monastery, learning to use your "bare hands", if you catch my drift.
So...lonely... and for what?
BWAAAAAAAAAAA!
There, there. It's not your fault your class fails to achieve its basic design intent.
Now get the hell out of here before a man with a REAL class decides to change the meaning of the phrase, "fighting unarmed".

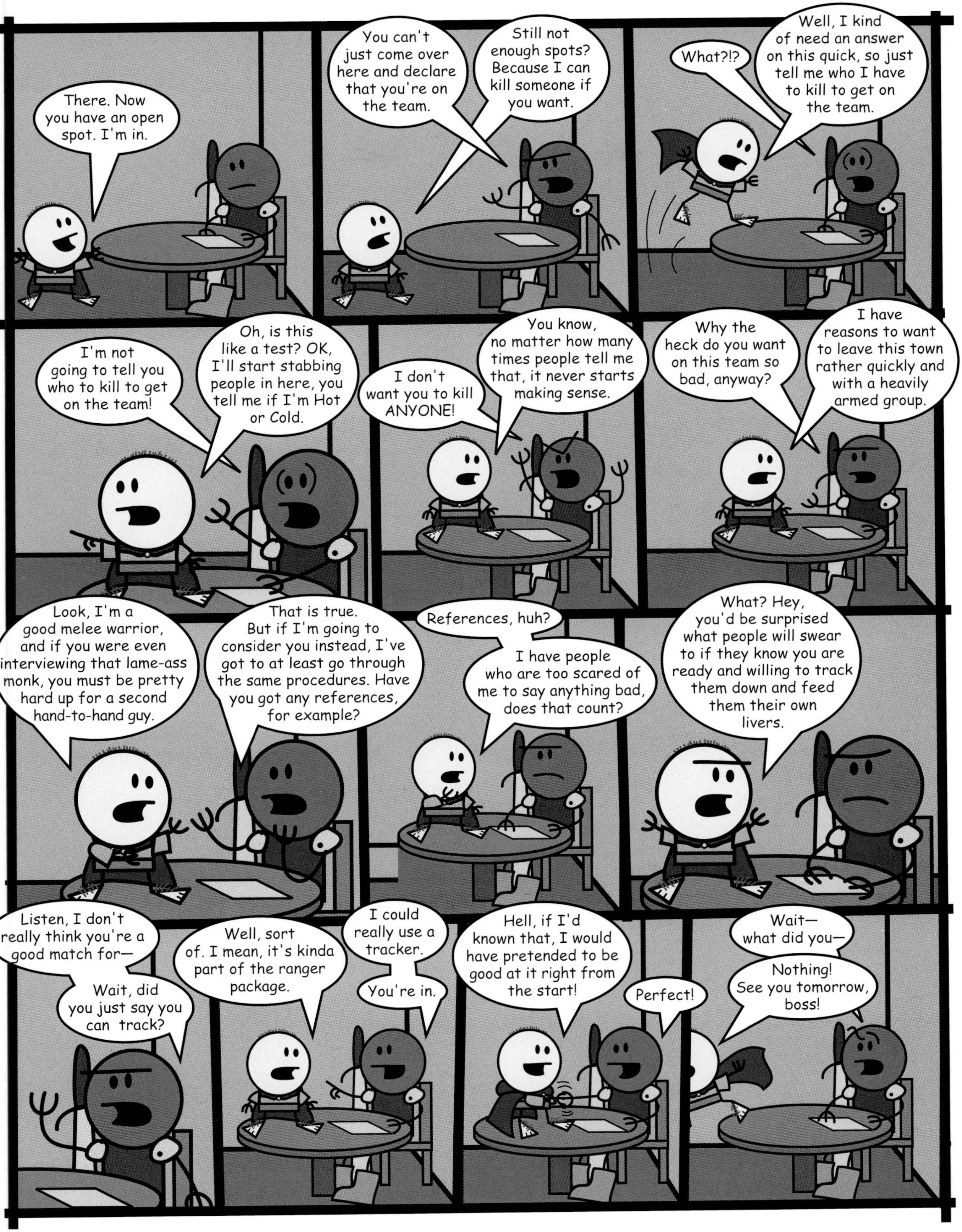
There. Now you have an open spot. I'm in.
You can't just come over here and declare that you're on the team.
Still not enough spots? Because I can kill someone if you want.
What?!?
Well, I kind of need an answer on this quick, so just tell me who I have to kill to get on the team.
I'm not going to tell you who to kill to get on the team!
Oh, is this like a test? OK, I'll start stabbing people in here, you tell me if I'm Hot or Cold.
I don't want you to kill ANYONE!
You know, no matter how many times people tell me that, it never starts making sense.
Why the heck do you want on this team so bad, anyway?
I have reasons to want to leave this town rather quickly and with a heavily armed group.
Look, I'm a good melee warrior, and if you were even interviewing that lame-ass monk, you must be pretty hard up for a second hand-to-hand guy.
That is true. But if I'm going to consider you instead, I've got to at least go through the same procedures. Have you got any references, for example?
References, huh?
I have people who are too scared of me to say anything bad, does that count?
What? Hey, you'd be surprised what people will swear to if they know you are ready and willing to track them down and feed them their own livers.
Listen, I don't really think you're a good match for—
Wait, did you just say you can track?
Well, sort of. I mean, it's kinda part of the ranger package.
I could really use a tracker.
You're in.
Hell, if I'd known that, I would have pretended to be good at it right from the start!
Perfect!
Wait— what did you—
Nothing! See you tomorrow, boss!

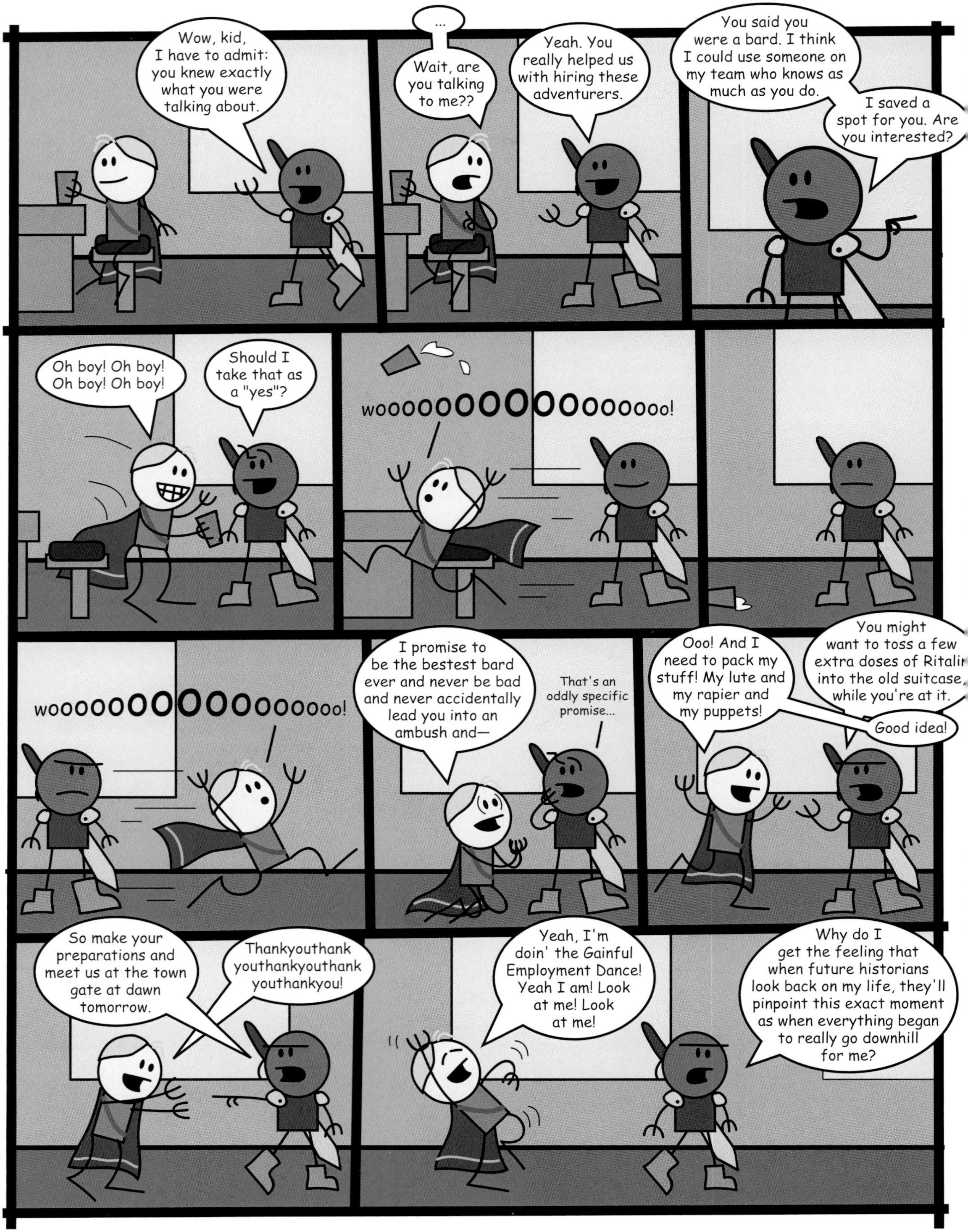
Wow, kid, I have to admit: you knew exactly what you were talking about.
...
Wait, are you talking to me??
Yeah. You really helped us with hiring these adventurers.
You said you were a bard. I think I could use someone on my team who knows as much as you do.
I saved a spot for you. Are you interested?
Oh boy! Oh boy! Oh boy! Oh boy!
Should I take that as a "yes"?
wooooooOOOOOoooooo!
woooooOOOOOoooooo!
I promise to be the bestest bard ever and never be bad and never accidentally lead you into an ambush and—
That's an oddly specific promise...
Ooo! And I need to pack my stuff! My lute and my rapier and my puppets!
You might want to toss a few extra doses of Ritalin into the old suitcase, while you're at it.
Good idea!
So make your preparations and meet us at the town gate at dawn tomorrow.
Thankyouthank youthankyouthank youthankyou!
Yeah, I'm doin' the Gainful Employment Dance! Yeah I am! Look at me! Look at me!
Why do I get the feeling that when future historians look back on my life, they'll pinpoint this exact moment as when everything began to really go downhill for me?

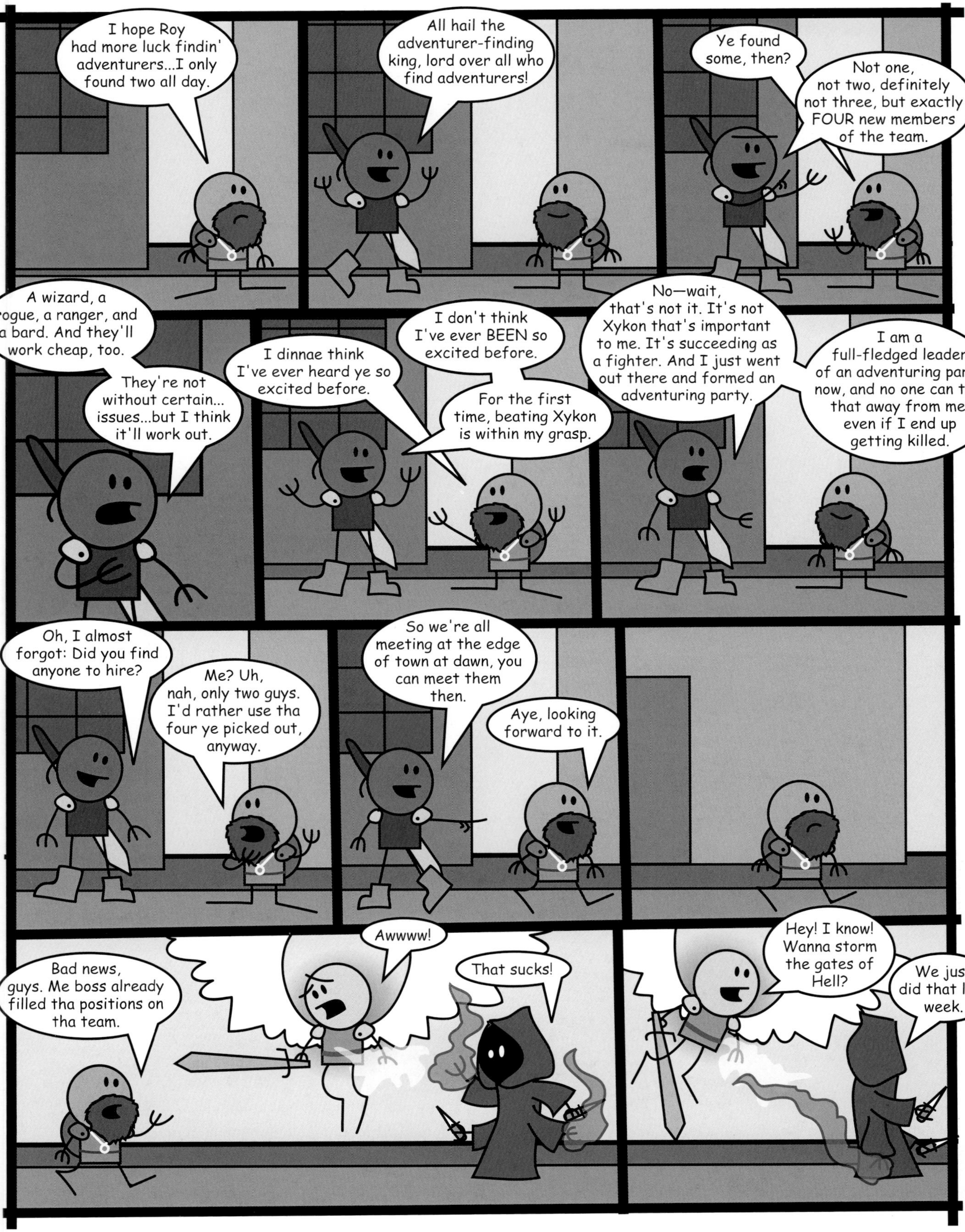
I hope Roy had more luck findin' adventurers...I only found two all day.
All hail the adventurer-finding king, lord over all who find adventurers!
Ye found some, then?
Not one, not two, definitely not three, but exactly FOUR new members of the team.
A wizard, a rogue, a ranger, and a bard. And they'll work cheap, too.
They're not without certain... issues...but I think it'll work out.
I dinnae think I've ever heard ye so excited before.
I don't think I've ever BEEN so excited before.
For the first time, beating Xykon is within my grasp.
No—wait, that's not it. It's not Xykon that's important to me. It's succeeding as a fighter. And I just went out there and formed an adventuring party.
I am a full-fledged leader of an adventuring party now, and no one can take that away from me, even if I end up getting killed.
Oh, I almost forgot: Did you find anyone to hire?
Me? Uh, nah, only two guys. I'd rather use tha four ye picked out, anyway.
So we're all meeting at the edge of town at dawn, you can meet them then.
Aye, looking forward to it.
Bad news, guys. Me boss already filled tha positions on tha team.
Awwww!
That sucks!
Hey! I know! Wanna storm the gates of Hell?
We just did that last week.

Yesterday

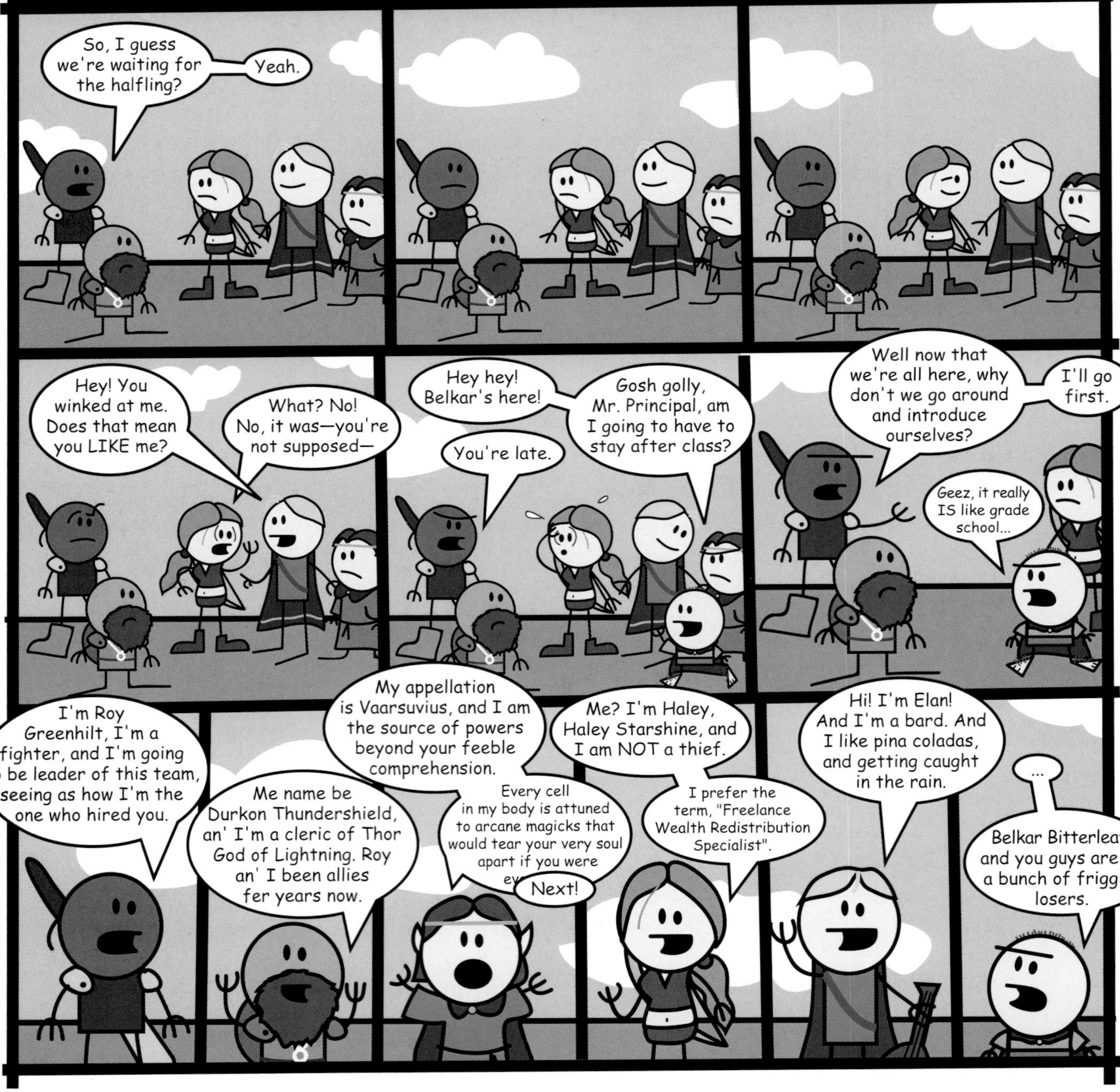
So, I guess we're waiting for the halfling?
Yeah.
Hey! You winked at me. Does that mean you LIKE me?
What? No! No, it was—you're not supposed—
Hey hey! Belkar's here!
You're late.
Gosh golly, Mr. Principal, am I going to have to stay after class?
Well now that we're all here, why don't we go around and introduce ourselves?
I'll go first.
Geez, it really IS like grade school...
I'm Roy Greenhilt, I'm a fighter, and I'm going to be leader of this team, seeing as how I'm the one who hired you.
Me name be Durkon Thundershield, an' I'm a cleric of Thor God of Lightning. Roy an' I been allies fer years now.
My appellation is Vaarsuvius, and I am the source of powers beyond your feeble comprehension.
Every cell in my body is attuned to arcane magicks that would tear your very soul apart if you were ev
Next!
Me? I'm Haley, Haley Starshine, and I am NOT a thief.
I prefer the term, "Freelance Wealth Redistribution Specialist".
Hi! I'm Elan! And I'm a bard. And I like pina coladas, and getting caught in the rain.
...
Belkar Bitterleaf, and you guys are all a bunch of friggin' losers.

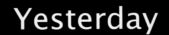

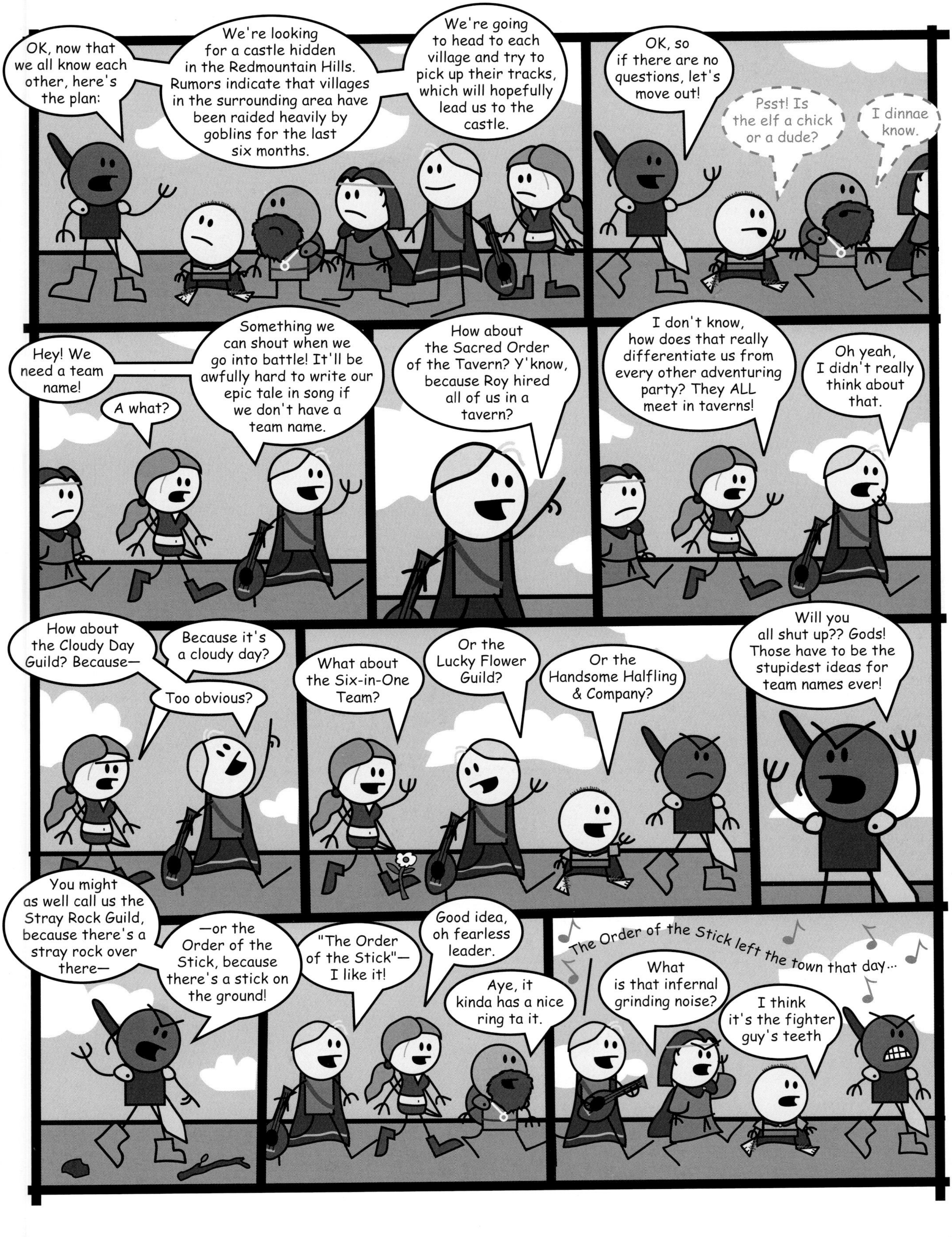
OK, now that we all know each other, here's the plan:
We're looking for a castle hidden in the Redmountain Hills. Rumors indicate that villages in the surrounding area have been raided heavily by goblins for the last six months.
We're going to head to each village and try to pick up their tracks, which will hopefully lead us to the castle.
OK, so if there are no questions, let's move out!
Psst! Is the elf a chick or a dude?
I dinnae know.
Hey! We need a team name!
A what?
Something we can shout when we go into battle! It'll be awfully hard to write our epic tale in song if we don't have a team name.
How about the Sacred Order of the Tavern? Y'know, because Roy hired all of us in a tavern?
I don't know, how does that really differentiate us from every other adventuring party? They ALL meet in taverns!
Oh yeah, I didn't really think about that.
How about the Cloudy Day Guild? Because—
Because it's a cloudy day?
Too obvious?
What about the Six-in-One Team?
Or the Lucky Flower Guild?
Or the Handsome Halfling & Company?
Will you all shut up?? Gods! Those have to be the stupidest ideas for team names ever!
You might as well call us the Stray Rock Guild, because there's a stray rock over there—
—or the Order of the Stick, because there's a stick on the ground!
"The Order of the Stick"— I like it!
Good idea, oh fearless leader.
Aye, it kinda has a nice ring ta it.
The Order of the Stick left the town that day...
What is that infernal grinding noise?
I think it's the fighter guy's teeth

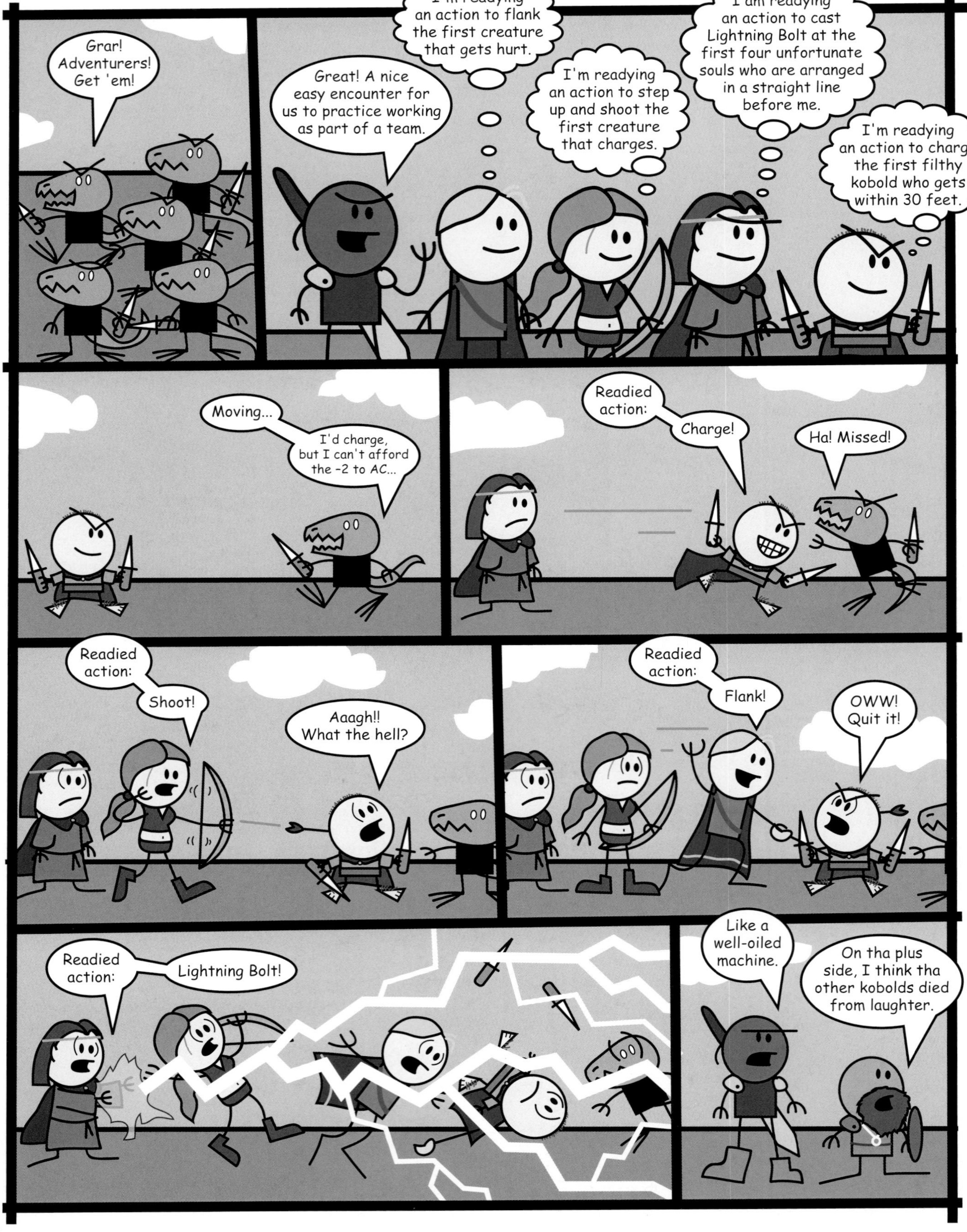
Grar! Adventurers! Get 'em!
Great! A nice easy encounter for us to practice working as part of a team.
I'm readying an action to flank the first creature that gets hurt.
I'm readying an action to step up and shoot the first creature that charges.
I am readying an action to cast Lightning Bolt at the first four unfortunate souls who are arranged in a straight line before me.
I'm readying an action to charge the first filthy kobold who gets within 30 feet.
Moving...
I'd charge, but I can't afford the -2 to AC...
Readied action:
Charge!
Ha! Missed!
Readied action:
Shoot!
Aaagh!! What the hell?
Readied action:
Flank!
OWW! Quit it!
Readied action:
Lightning Bolt!
Like a well-oiled machine.
On tha plus side, I think tha other kobolds died from laughter.

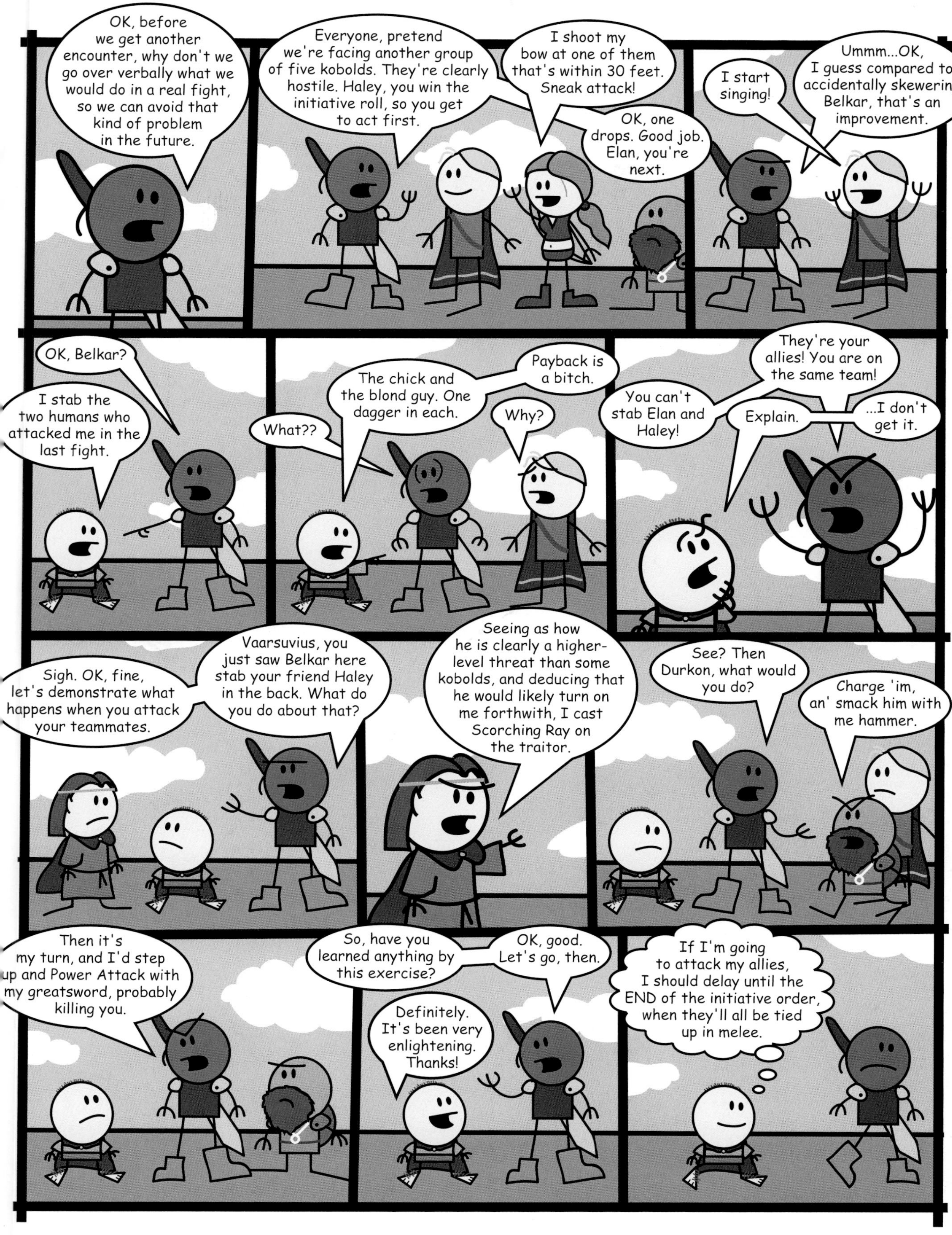

OK, before we get another encounter, why don't we go over verbally what we would do in a real fight, so we can avoid that kind of problem in the future.
Everyone, pretend we're facing another group of five kobolds. They're clearly hostile. Haley, you win the initiative roll, so you get to act first.
I shoot my bow at one of them that's within 30 feet. Sneak attack!
OK, one drops. Good job. Elan, you're next.
I start singing!
Ummm...OK, I guess compared to accidentally skewering Belkar, that's an improvement.
OK, Belkar?
I stab the two humans who attacked me in the last fight.
The chick and the blond guy. One dagger in each.
Payback is a bitch.
What??
Why?
You can't stab Elan and Haley!
They're your allies! You are on the same team!
Explain.
...I don't get it.
Sigh. OK, fine, let's demonstrate what happens when you attack your teammates.
Vaarsuvius, you just saw Belkar here stab your friend Haley in the back. What do you do about that?
Seeing as how he is clearly a higher-level threat than some kobolds, and deducing that he would likely turn on me forthwith, I cast Scorching Ray on the traitor.
See? Then Durkon, what would you do?
Charge 'im, an' smack him with me hammer.
Then it's my turn, and I'd step up and Power Attack with my greatsword, probably killing you.
So, have you learned anything by this exercise?
Definitely. It's been very enlightening. Thanks!
OK, good. Let's go, then.
If I'm going to attack my allies, I should delay until the END of the initiative order, when they'll all be tied up in melee.

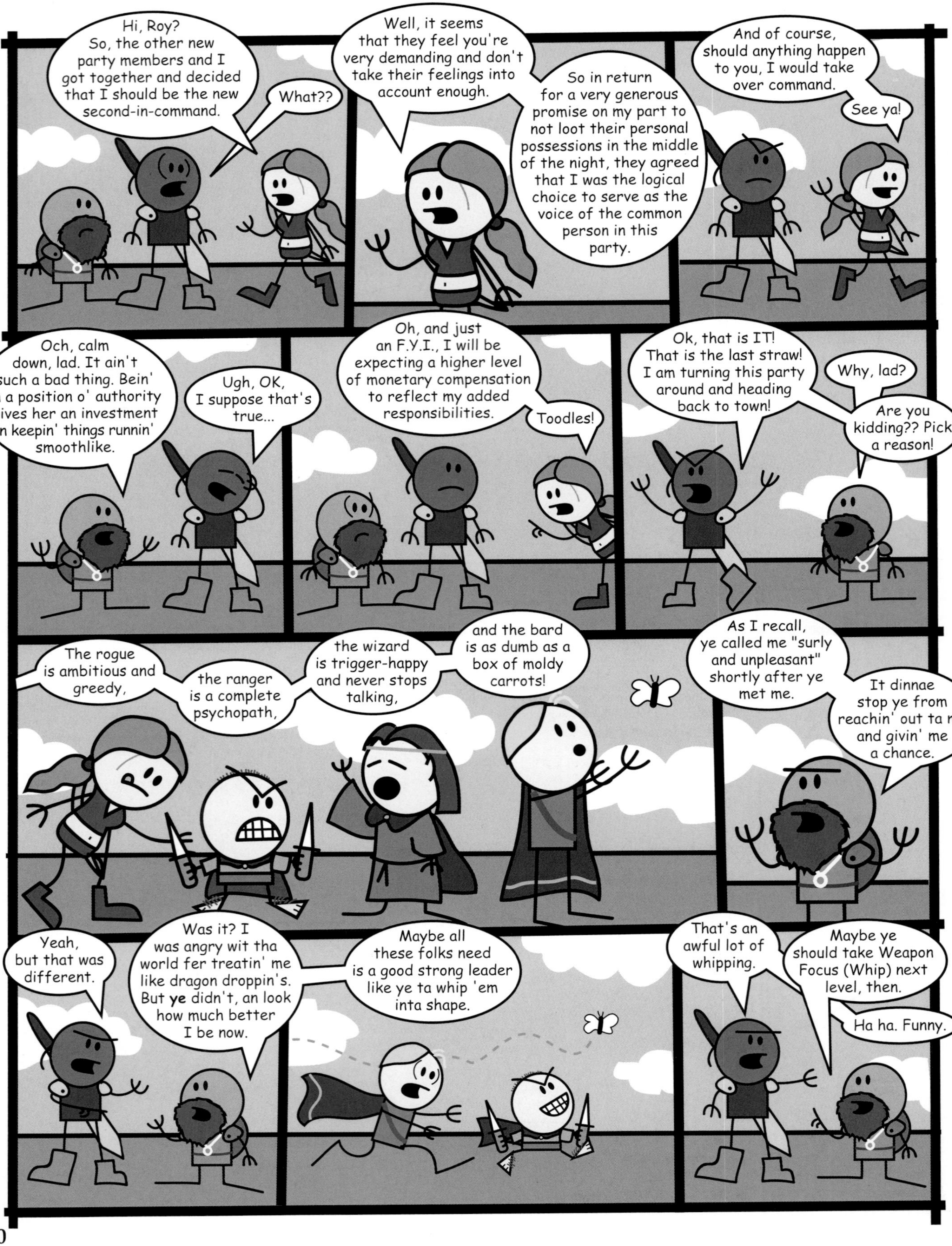
Hi, Roy? So, the other new party members and I got together and decided that I should be the new second-in-command.
What??
Well, it seems that they feel you're very demanding and don't take their feelings into account enough.
So in return for a very generous promise on my part to not loot their personal possessions in the middle of the night, they agreed that I was the logical choice to serve as the voice of the common person in this party.
And of course, should anything happen to you, I would take over command.
See ya!
Och, calm down, lad. It ain't such a bad thing. Bein' in a position o' authority gives her an investment in keepin' things runnin' smoothlike.
Ugh, OK, I suppose that's true...
Oh, and just an F.Y.I., I will be expecting a higher level of monetary compensation to reflect my added responsibilities.
Toodles!
Ok, that is IT! That is the last straw! I am turning this party around and heading back to town!
Why, lad?
Are you kidding?? Pick a reason!
The rogue is ambitious and greedy,
the ranger is a complete psychopath,
the wizard is trigger-happy and never stops talking,
and the bard is as dumb as a box of moldy carrots!
As I recall, ye called me "surly and unpleasant" shortly after ye met me.
It dinnae stop ye from reachin' out ta me and givin' me a chance.
Yeah, but that was different.
Was it? I was angry wit tha world fer treatin' me like dragon droppin's. But **ye** didn't, an look how much better I be now.
Maybe all these folks need is a good strong leader like ye ta whip 'em inta shape.
That's an awful lot of whipping.
Maybe ye should take Weapon Focus (Whip) next level, then.
Ha ha. Funny.

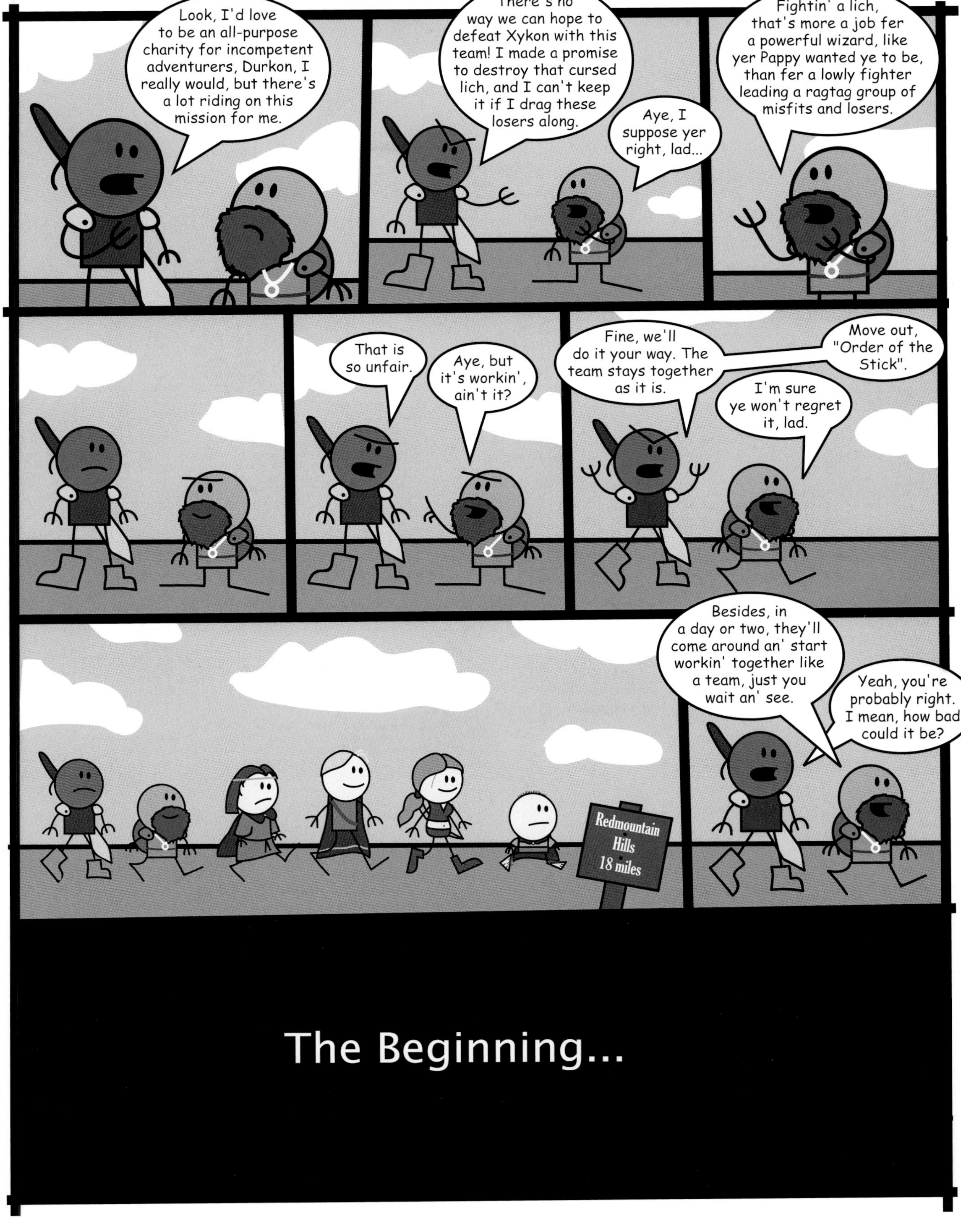
Look, I'd love to be an all-purpose charity for incompetent adventurers, Durkon, I really would, but there's a lot riding on this mission for me.
There's no way we can hope to defeat Xykon with this team! I made a promise to destroy that cursed lich, and I can't keep it if I drag these losers along.
Aye, I suppose yer right, lad...
Fightin' a lich, that's more a job fer a powerful wizard, like yer Pappy wanted ye to be, than fer a lowly fighter leading a ragtag group of misfits and losers.
That is so unfair.
Aye, but it's workin', ain't it?
Fine, we'll do it your way. The team stays together as it is.
Move out, "Order of the Stick".
I'm sure ye won't regret it, lad.
Redmountain Hills 18 miles
Besides, in a day or two, they'll come around an' start workin' together like a team, just you wait an' see.
Yeah, you're probably right. I mean, how bad could it be?
The Beginning...

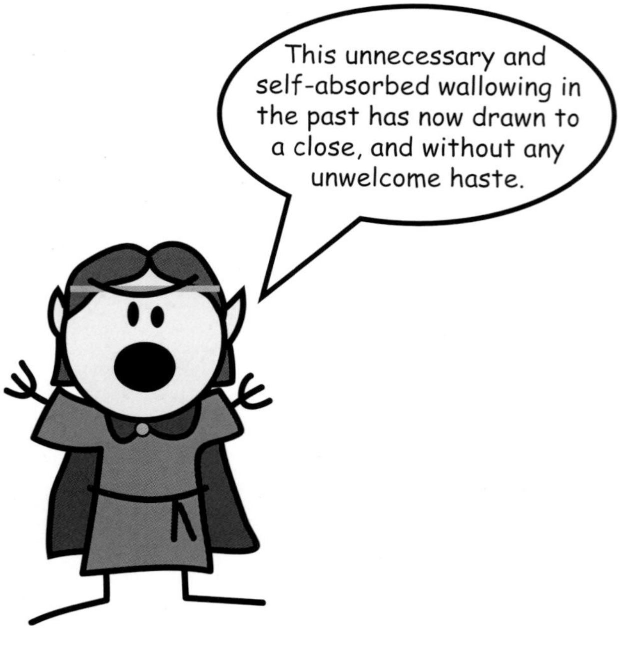
This unnecessary and self-absorbed wallowing in the past has now drawn to a close, and without any unwelcome haste.